Real Characters, Places and Most Unusual Things!

Serving Home Builders Since 1912

Savannah PLANING MILL CO.

Lumber and Service

WHEATON and LIBERTY STREETS
SAVANNAH, GEORGIA

SINCE 1912
PHONE 2-7168 P. O. BOX 114

Close Cover Before Striking

Real Characters, Places and Most Unusual Things!

HOOCHIE-COOCHIE TUNA FIRE TAIL!

A Daughter's Greatest Tales!

Gangsters, heroes, watchers,
hijackers, fishers, funerals,
mayhem, murder, lies, and fighting!

By Captain Judy Helmey
"Kicking Fish Tail Since 1956!"

Typesetting and Design by:

Lauren Clackum
Pacific Publishers, LLC
PO Box 2813, Tybee Island, Georgia 31328

Print ISBN: 979-8-88617-067-2

Printed in the United States of America

A big thanks goes out to the many great friends that helped me with this endeavor!

~ **Captain Judy Helmey** ~
2025

CAPTAIN JUDY HELMEY
60 years taking customers fishing and still going!

What is this book about?

Captain Judy says and does the darndest things!
"Kicking Fish Tail Since 1956!"

Short stories about sunken ships, mermaids, Al Capone, both parent's funerals, Ours and their submarines, fishing, my father's 8 wives, my 6 stepmothers, murder, lies told, mayhem, cold cases, my father's crazy life before me, life on Wilmington Island with me, and ours together! My father's very interesting life offered me plenty of things to write about! It's best described as a daughter's greatest tale!

What has happened since I published My Father the Sea and Me in 1992. We officially came up with "Kicking Fish Tails Since 1956!" And then I had it trademarked! Everyone always asks, "Why 1956?" That is the year that I officially started fishing with my father on his big wooden boat. After my mother died in a car accident in 1957 my father's wooden boat became officially Captain Helmey's Day Care on the sea for me! My father's wooden boat was 41 feet Long, it had a big stateroom, two heads with showers, a dining room, big galley, a big dash at the helm where I could fit just nicely, and basically lots of places to roam. I was a happy camper!

TABLE OF CONTENTS

MY MOTHER!

I must start somewhere, so I will start with my mother being killed in 1957. Let me throw a few dates out so that you can get the just of the situation.

My mother moved to Savannah a couple of years before she met my father. (Sherman I. Helmey) She got a job at the telephone company, which was located on Drayton Street in Downtown Savannah. She and a few other workers rented a house on one of the state's streets by Bonaventure. What are the state's streets? It is an area where all streets are named after states, like Florida, Texas, Alabama Pennsylvania etc.

My father told me that he had seen my mother crossing the street in front of the Telephone company. And when he passed her, he told the friend in the car with him, that this was the women he was going to marry! And he did!

My father Captain Sherman I. Helmey (1900-1993), age 44 married my mother Geraldine (Jerry) Lovitt Helmey (1925-1957) in 1946 at the age of 22. I was born in 1951, and my mother was killed in a very awful car accident in 1957.

Just the other day...

I had a charter fishing customer call me wanting information. He asked me if I knew where Reidsville, Georgia was located and I replied yes, but for unsettling reasons. I told the customer that my mother was killed in a very bad automobile accident in 1957 in Reidsville, Georgia. It was said that the mayor's wife hit us.

And it turned into a Perry Mason Trial for sure. And just like that Tom (not his real name) said, "The mayor's name is (not filling this blank in!) and I heard that the mayor's wife was drinking as well as driving at a high rate of speed!" And then I said, "Ditches were dug, and ditches were covered up!"

Tom said, "As a small child I had ears and that is what I heard!" Once again Disney was right, "It's a small, small world after all!"

My mother's younger sister "Suggie" took the picture to the right on our dock in July 1956. She found it in 1996 and sent it to me! In November 1957 my mother was killed in an awful car accident in Reidsville, Georgia!

I was right at six years old when my mother was killed. This happened on my birthday!

On a happier note: During this time my father would go catch the live shrimp and my mother would sell them from our dock! According to my father, my mother had lots of business!

*Topless Little Miss Judy was 5 years old
when this picture was taken!*

*This is my mother pumping gas into my father's boat.
She not only sold live shrimp, but she also sold gas and diesel!*

3

My Mother's Burial and Some Greatly Cherished Pictures!

I guess all children's memories commence at different times. In my case, my memories began right after my mother was killed in an automobile accident, which happened around my sixth birthday. The fact of the matter is, it was on the date of my birthday, which is November 13. Although this was a very sad time, life has a way of moving on no matter what.

This is not a picture of the actual car, but this is exactly what I remember as a child. Large white wall tires and shiny new wooden sides panels!

It's funny what you remember about your own past. I can remember the car accident as if it happened only yesterday. I don't remember my mother in the car so much, but only after she was thrown out of the car. I do remember her screaming "Sherman watch out!"

And then I remember finding her on the ground quite a distance from the car that we had just got out of. A man driving a station wagon with wooden panels down the sides stopped to help us.

I would later in life realize that they called this station wagon a "woody." We put my mother in the back of the station wagon, and I watched from the front seat as she wiggled a little side to side. There was a lot of blood coming from her head and mouth area, but it seemed she was still trying to speak. After leaving the hospital in Reidsville, Georgia I found out just by listening that my mother had bit her tongue off and the back of her was crushed!

Before we left the hospital, I remember playing in the waiting room. The floors were covered in big black and white squares. I tried every which way to walk on them without stepping on the cracks. After all, stepping on a crack would break your mother's back and she was having enough trouble.

Black and white squares! Don't step on the cracks!

My father had been gone for a while, and I was making the best of the situation. Even though I didn't know there would not be a good ending! My father walked in, asked if I would like to see my mother and of course I ran to him with a smile.

However, he was not smiling, and he had sadness on his face that I had not ever seen before. He picked me up and as we entered the room, I saw my mother with her head all bandaged up. I tried to talk to her, but she did not answer, nor did she move.

I have always wondered if I was looking at my mother after she had passed.

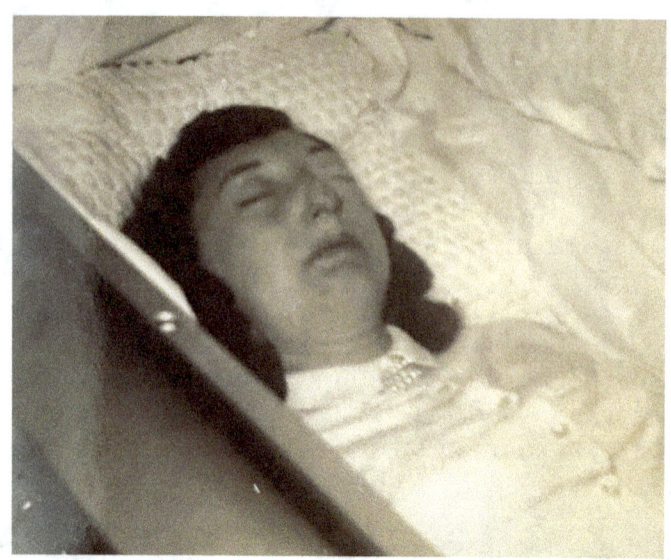

My mother, Geraldine Lovitt Helmey (1925-1957)
better known as Jerry!

I guess you could say it is a southern tradition to take pictures of our loved ones while they lay to rest in their casket. Here is a picture of my mother in her casket. Being I was only 6 years only when all this picture taking happened, I was not the one that performed this task.

It is funny but as I look at all these flowers, I can remember that the funeral home was packed full of people! My mother's funeral was handled by Henderson Brothers and ended up costing $1040.00!

My mother posed for the camera while my father took this picture! I bet this grown was purchased at Fines Department store!

My mother once again posing in the same place in her new fur coat that I can only assume was purchased at Kirschner Furs. (Established 1895)

As a child I heard about Kirschner furs all the time. And since my father always proclaimed he gave all his women a Cadillac and a fur coat. I assume all furs were purchased at Kirschner's and all Cadillac's at Backus!

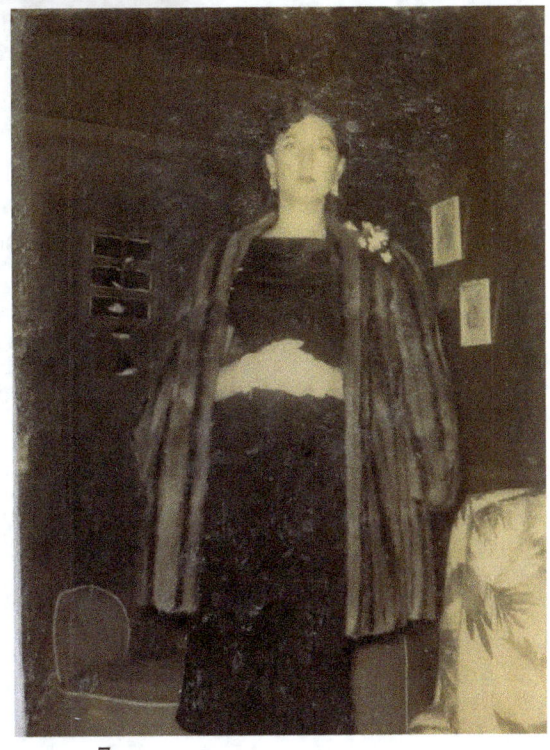

This is my mother in the summer of 1956 at the Oglethorpe Hotel, which is located on the beautiful Wilmington River! During this time, we were members of the hotel's yacht club, which meant, I think, that we got to use the pool.

In my case, at 5 years old a pool was an important thing and so was the high dive. The pool was great! It was big, deep, and it had two diving boards. There was the regular height diving board and then there was the high dive.

Now, I can't tell you the height of this, but it was darn high especially to a 5-year-old. However, that never stopped me from running and jumping off the high dive!

This is my mother and father with friends. I was either not born yet or somewhere taking a nap. I believe this is one of those pictures where drinking might have been involved!

My father always said, "Your mother was a tall drink of water!" Well, as you can see, he was right for sure!

I do not have a lot of pictures of my mother. Most of the pictures I do have were taken in Greenwich Cemetery, which is where she was, shortly thereafter laid to rest!

My mother, once again, at someone's grave in Greenwich cemetery posing for the camera!

10

Once again, my mother was posing for this picture. Now I do believe that a real photographer took this picture. I am assuming Olin Mills! The back of the photo didn't reveal that information, but it certainly looks like their work for sure! My mother was around until my sixth birthday and then she was killed in a serious car accident. Now, isn't it funny that I have several pictures of her that are taken in the cemetery? And you are not going to believe this one. At the time, my father had not purchased any burial plots. These pictures were taken in Greenwich Cemetery sometimes between the years 1951 to 1956. When my mother was killed (car accident) in 1957, he brought burial plots in this cemetery. In 1957 the cost of 4 burial lots in Greenwich Cemetery was $226.00.

Once again, my mother is posing in the same cemetery that she would shortly be laid to rest in. The fact of the matter is you can see exactly where she is buried now, which is a little to the left of the big oak tree in the top right section of this picture! What's even more odd is the fact that the Helmey tombstone now looks just like the one shown in this picture.

I think my mother was very beautiful! And if I knew her very much, I know I would have missed her more!

This next picture was lost many years after my mother passed away. One day right after her death it was in the house and the next minute it was not. It showed back up in mid-nineties. On this day, Captain Kathy Brown was straightening a framed picture that was hanging on the wall in the living room. As soon as she put her hand on the bottom of the frame two pictures fell out from behind the picture right into the cup of her hand. I wish I had a picture of Kathy's face when this happened. We both examined the picture frame, and neither could one of us found an opening behind the current picture in the frame nor could be able to find a hole in the wall. The other piece that fell out was a picture of my father and his business partner/friend Pete Hudson!

And then the night before the pictures fell out of the wall, Captain Kathy's mother Mrs. Wilma in the wee morning had a tap on her shoulder. According to the story told, a figure resembling my mother told Mrs. Wilma that she appreciates her being here!

A medium told me many years ago that we had a happy spirit living in our house. I never mentioned to the Medium that I had seen the whisk of my mother dozens of times in the house. And there are several stories in this book about Frances Cochran. She worked for us as a housekeeper and caretaker of mine for many years. I truly believe that my mother and Mrs. Cochran had a conversation about me! (Captain Judy) Why do I think that? Mrs. Cochran did not know our family before she arrived at our house to work for us. It is like she came to work for us with complete knowledge of everything about me.

13

Little Miss Judy is standing by her father's 1957 Ford Fairlane.

This was the car that my mother was thrown from after it spun like a top on its back wheel. Although not shown, the right corner panel has been replaced and is still unpainted! According to paperwork that I have found, it costs $1,063.26 to repair this car. The 1957 Ford Fairlane, when it was brand new, sold for around $1960.00. I don't know if you have been keeping up with my stories, but in this picture, I am really dressed up and instead of having black patten leather shoes on I am wearing white patten leather shoes! A girl got to change up!

AFTER MY MOTHER'S FUNERAL SERVICES... THE LAWSUIT!

After the funeral services were held and all the court room drama of who was to blame for the accident was played out Perry Mason style my memories began...

I don't want you to get bored with all the details, but in August 1958 my father was sued by the person driving the car that hit us. When my mother got killed in November 1957, my father was trying to make a left-hand turn and had almost made it having his front tires off the pavement.

The lady who was suing us, better known as the Plaintiff, wants restitution for her pain and suffering! According to her doctors, the Plaintiff was seriously, painfully and permanently injured as follows: severe injuries to right leg, with residual edema, a hard swollen areas below the knee, an ulcer and skin rash attributable to said injury; laceration of right forehead, with bruising of right supraorbital nerve and residual disturbance of sensation to right forehead; neck injuries, with mal alignment of cervical spine with resultant tenderness, pain on motion and excruciating headaches, requiring further treatment by cervical traction and hospitalization; extreme nervousness, impairing Plaintiff's ability to perform her usual and customary duties. All injuries are supposedly permanent in nature!

But I have to say, "My mother injuries were so permanent that she died from them!"

I copied this from the old trial records from the courthouse, which I have thoroughly read more than once. I especially found the examination of the plaintiff truly interesting for all the wrong reasons. After reading her deposition, it was clear that this woman was driving in an alcoholic black out. She hit our car while making way at about 65 plus MPH. She never braked, she never swerved, and I truly don't believe she knew that she was in an accident.

15

My father, who was about 57-year-old at this time, found himself now raising a 6-year-old daughter alone with all the trimmings. These short stories that I have written are all about my father's life before and after he married my mother. We had one heck of a time trying to move forward as a family. They are funny and oh so true.

The bottom line is that these short stories reveal one heck of tale that needs to be shared by all. To say that this book has been written with a no literary standard meaning I should have listened more while in my English class. And some say, "I do a great job of murdering the King's English!" (Captain Dick "Pops" Howell was the one person that said this the most, but he always had a big smile on his face! He was a skilled and knowledgeable college English professor!) I have been told by many that my writing is not professional. However, I have also been told by many more that I truly do have my own style of writing, and they love to read my stories. The best thing that I can tell you is I have tried compiling all of daddy's stories, my life experiences, into a writing form so that you could understand, and this was quite difficult. So, I got to thinking with all these things that I must just write my way using my best method. So, I have old pictures from my father's past, pictures given to me, and those that I have taken myself! And in some cases, the best way to tell a story is picture by picture.

As far as the stories go... I would like to say in my defense that some of these stories are second hand. I have either heard them from friends or straight from the horse's mouth, which in this case was my father. My father was 51 years old when I was born. So therefore I, Captain Judy, never allegedly hauled any illegal shipments of any type during the thirties. There is a good reason! I wasn't born until 1951!

I will start off by saying, "My father started this charter boat company in 1948, and I started fishing with him in 1956!" Thus, the real honest to goodness "Kicking Fish Tail Since 1956!" was put into effect!

In 2024 I was inducted into the Georgia Outdoor Writers Fishing and Hunting Hall of Fame! This truly was an honor for me!

I say, "The heck with the king's English!" I have done it my way!

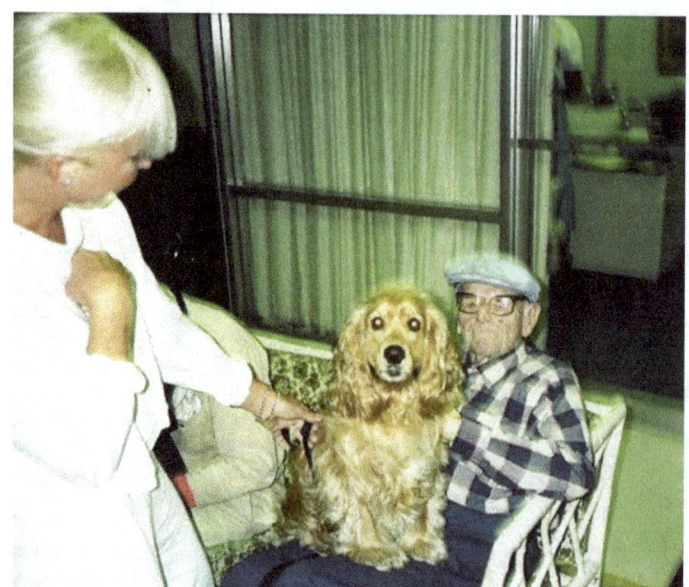

Captain Sherman I. Helmey is visiting with his new friend!
The greatest Cocker spaniel ever! She loved the patients at
the nursing home, and they loved her!

Captain Sherman I. Helmey, my father, loved teddy bears.
And we would always get him a teddy bear for any reason!

18

DADDY'S FUNERAL

I should start all my stories out with, "You are not going to believe this one!" And this story is no different.

After a long illness while staying in the nursing home my father passed peacefully on Thursday March 11, 1993. My father suffered from brain apathy, which is like Alzheimer, but caused from excessive drinking.

Now, when I say excessive drinking, you must be thinking that my father was a drinker from morning to night and he never stopped. Well, that could not be further from the truth. The fact of the matter is he would only drink after 5 PM. Now I will say, "It might have been a fifth of liquor downing before he departed for his outing on the town."

He always said, "A person that starts drinking before 5 PM could be a considered an alcoholic." Oh my!

So therefore, when you consume large amounts of liquor sooner or later it is going to start destroying brain cells. At the ripe old age of 93 years of age, my father went to the big fishing pond in the sky!

As with everything else my father did, there were always sparks and mayhem running array. And his death either brought it on or it was coming anyway, which was later titled "the storm of the century!"

Greenwich Cemetery located in Thunderbolt, Georgia;
located behind Bonaventure Cemetery.

NOT ENOUGH ROOM
AT THE HELMEY PLOT FOR DADDY!

This is where daddy was supposed to be laid to rest! However, after our first observation, some changes and removals had to take place.

Before my father passed, I had already taken care of all the details of his funeral. All I really had to do was contact Fox and the week's funeral home to get time to meet someone at the Helmey grave site. My appointment was for 9 AM and I was supposed to show the burial person where I wanted daddy to be placed. I arrived at the grave first, which meant for a minute, it was extra quiet. Then a truck pulled up and the older man getting out introduced himself as Mr. Eufonious Johnson. We shaked hands and I started pointing the area that I wanted daddy placed.

Mr. Johnson pulled out his long metal T-bar and started poking the ground at least a good 5 feet. Some of the pronging's met with no resistance, but then the end of the bar hit something. I didn't think much of it until Mr. Johnson said, "This spot is taken!" At this point, I didn't know what to say other than to suggest moving over a bit.

ONE REGULAR BURIAL
AND ONE NOT SO REGULAR!

There were no headstones over these graves, and I knew why for one, but not the other. And the other was something that I hadn't talked about to anyone for a long time. And the ones standing at the grave didn't know either.

According to Eufonious, there was a smaller casket and then there was, at least it seemed like a wooden casket. I just stood there and Eufonious said, "I have got to go back to the office to tell them about my findings! I am sure this is a mistake and can be straighten out quickly!"

As I watched Mr. Johnson drive off my mind went in reverse, and it stopped when it reached 23 years back. During this time, I had a little girl, which we named Jerry Lynn Helmey Jones. She was very premature and did not live, but for a few hours. It was a very sad event; she was so small. I remained in the hospital and daddy handled everything.

For some reason and although it was not a secret, I had chosen to keep this information locked in and never really shared it with anyone.

As far as the other grave that had been placed next to my mother, which was where I was going to place my father, I didn't have a clue or did I? And then my mind started searching again in reverse.

Believe me, when this happens, I know, something is going to surface in my memory that maybe I wanted to forget.

And just like that, a thought popped into my head. I remember a late night in 1968 when my father had told me that Janet possibly had been murdered.

WHO IS JANET?

Ok, who is Janet? Not sure if she is wife number 5 or just a common law thing. However, it was known far and wide that my father and Janet were a couple. It was not because they were admired, it was that they had been thrown out of every fine restaurant in Savannah.

The restaurant owners would always tell daddy, "Mr. Helmey this is not because of you, I do this, because of your guest!" As you already know was Janet!

Janet was a wild one and when you add alcohol to this mix you get all kinds of nasty actions! When all the food, plates, drinks, and anything else that wasn't attached in proximity became airborne it was necessary to remove this bad-tempered violet woman!

In other words when other patrons in the establishment started complaining and then feared being in the same room with this crazy person changes had to be made.

With all this happening repeatedly, a bad reputation gets had. And bad news travels faster in some cases than the good stuff! If I tried to share all the bad stuff that Janet did at our house, we would be here for a while.

However, I can't go on with this true story without giving you some of the facts. And I always plan to say, "This stuff is way too good to have made up!"

Janet was shorter than most of the ladies that daddy dated. However, she was very beautiful sporting a head with thick long black hair.

The longer you knew her the more things you could add to her list of MO'S! (*Modus operandi* Latin phase for "ways of operating!")

My father should have purchased stock from the Yellow Cab Company! After all the money he spent on transportation for Janet and outside deliveries made he would have made a solid investment!

I am sure somewhere in all this information I might have mentioned Janet, when in confrontation mode, would always take her clothes off. I remember this one daytime incident where Janet had taken her clothes off, daddy was trying to put her into the cab, but once he shut the door she would jump over into the front seat and back out!

It certainly was not comical then, but now some fifty plus years later I am smiling about it. You know there are some things that you can't get out of your head. In my case, why not get some fun out of these crazy memories!

Yellow Cab Era!

Janet did not drive! It was either because Janet didn't have a license, or she didn't know how. So therefore, when Janet made a move, she obtained the services of a Yellow Cab! So therefore, if a Yellow Cab was seen in our yard, especially in my case, it was time to take cover. Why? Janet was on the property and about to do something bad!

There was this one time that Janet broke most of the windows located on the dirt road driveway side of our house. How? There was a convenience stack of solid red bricks near the house. She turned these handheld bricks into some serious throwing projectiles. And this was the era before double-planned hurricane rated windows were made available. So, you must know the bricks easily broke the windows and came flying right into the house! As soon as Janet was tired of throwing bricks and breaking windows, she grabbed her waiting yellow cab and made a safe get away! I must say, "Storm Janet would make a great test person for throwing bricks at hurricane rated windows!"

And then there was that time were Janet broke into the house poured red fingernail polish all over kitchen floor. As if this wasn't enough, she then poured coffee grinds on top of the nail polish. Now I know you are wondering if the Yellow Cab driver and Janet had something going on. Well, who knows this point? However, the cab driver never knew what was going on! Why? Janet had him pull up the driveway and wait for her. And of course, I forgot to mention this, but daddy had set up an account for Janet at the Yellow Cab Company! Boy oh boy, I didn't see the bill, but I heard somewhat about it!

The Yellow Cab Company didn't just drive Janet where she wanted to go, they also delivered too. What did they deliver? Food and beverages such as beer and liquor. And you thought Uber Eats, Door Dash, and Grubhub were new ideas. Heck, Janet had it going on in the sixties!!! When Janet stayed at our house, if she ran out of adult beverages or cigarettes, the Yellow

Cab company was called, and it was shortly delivered!

Well, there was one time when my father and I had a fishing charter, which meant we would be gone from the house at least 10 hours. It was also one of those times when Janet was visiting! One the way to the boat, neither one of us talked about the possibilities of what Janet might do, because it was way too late in the game to worry about that.

Captain Judy Helmey and father Captain Sherman I. Helmey.
All dressed up and ready to go!

Old Time Lazaretto Creek Bridge and Cockspur Lighthouse Picture

This picture was taken by Captain Elizabeth and Captain Cecil Johnson, long time owners of Tybee Island Charters! This photo was most likely taken during the fifties/sixties while standing on the Lazaretto Creek Bridge located on Tybee Island also known as Savannah Beach, Georgia. Captain Charles Walsh operated this dock for many years. Then his son Captain Bill Walsh took over for many more years. When the Walsh's were done it became the current home for Captain Derek Brown's Dolphin Magic Tours accommodating his many big tours and fishing boats. (Look them up and take a dolphin tour!)

In the background is the Cockspur Lighthouse, which was built in 1854. It is still standing today and has had a great facelift! Look it up!

HUMAN CHUM BASKET

The first boat, Miss Jerry, is tied to the outside of the dock. She is a wooden boat that my father and I worked on for many years. See the raft located on the top of his boat? Well, back in the fifties/sixties this raft was called the "chum basket!" and for good reasons too. It was made of hard plastic, which means in the water during rough sea conditions you could hit your head, meaning not a good situation. So called lifelines were hanging off the side of the float and those in the water were supposed to hang on. In the middle of the raft was netting that would hold water and supplies. This was called the Chum Basket part of the raft! This orange hard plastic USCG approved life raft was supposed to support 15 souls while they were hanging on in the water. I am happy to report that we never had to use this USCG raft aka chum basket!

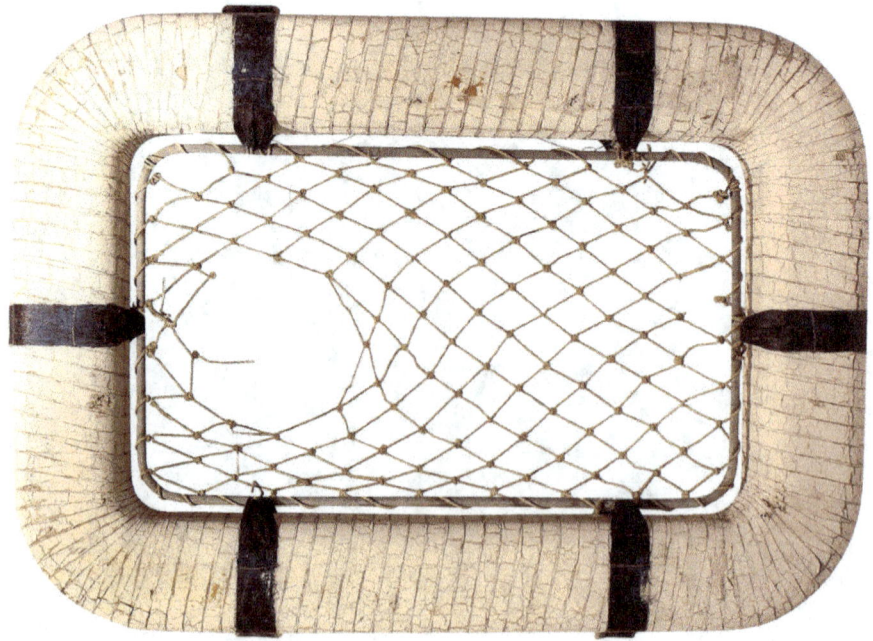

BACK TO THE STORY... WIG WEARING TIME!

After a long day in the ocean, and after cleaning the boats up, we headed home. When we arrived at the door facing the creek, daddy unlocked it, but it would not open. He looked puzzled because he knew the door was unlocked. So, we started pushing on it. And it finally moved. When we got the door open enough to stick our heads in, we found Janet passed out on the floor up against the door. Basically, our doorstop was a fall-down drunk passed out Janet! So, we tried to get Janet up, but she would not respond. Heck, for a moment we thought she might be dead, but then she started moving.

As Janet haphazardly sat up, the towel around her head loosened up. And that's when I smelled a strong odor of some sort of Clorox or peroxide. When Janet removed the towel, I wasn't ready for what I was seeing. Janet had put some sort of peroxide Lightner on her hair. Then she drank until she passed out, but that must have been hours ago! Her black hair was sort of dirty blonde, and it was basically falling out. I decided it was time for me to go to my room!

Somehow, Janet cut her hair very short and then it became wig wearing time! Well, I am sure you as a reader can figure out what happened. Well, of course Janet ran out of beer/liquor, and she called Yellow Cab to make a delivery. However, she added some sort of hydrogen peroxide to the list of things to bring. So therefore, when the Yellow Cab company arrived Janet must have started drinking and poured all the supposed hair lighten ingredients on head. Then she passed out and the rest is losing her hair history!

I don't know if I had mentioned this or not but by trade Janet was a hairdresser. She was supposed to know about this stuff. Maybe when the hair stuff was delivered, she was too drunk to read the label so therefore she skipped that part and basically just dumped it on her head. From the looks of her head, she must have rubbed it in also! We know you shouldn't drink and drive, but now we need to add don't get buzzed and try to color your hair!

29

SCREEN DOOR SHUFFLE

I remember this one night it seemed very peaceful around the house. And then suddenly, I heard screaming and lots of bumping noises coming from daddy's end of the house. Then the noise seemed like it was getting closer.

I jumped up and sure enough Janet was headed my way with knife in hand with daddy drafting right behind her. She had already stabbed Daddy; I could see blood running from his chest. I slammed my bedroom door and quickly locked it. And that was right before Janet ran into it. There was a loud BAM and then I heard Daddy and Janet screaming at each other!

When I finally felt like I could safely open my door, I did. Daddy and Janet were pushing each other around. Daddy basically threw Janet out of the top section of the screen door. And then as if that hadn't even taken place she came back with more fury, knife in hand, through the bottom of the door. It was time to slam my bedroom door again and maybe come up with a plan to get the heck out of here!

Then as if not a thing had happened there was silence again. I opened my door and saw daddy standing over a wig-less wearing naked woman better known as Janet! She was either knocked out by daddy or she just plain passed out. I didn't ask! I was just glad this short violet war was over at least for the moment!

The Call!

I was about 16 years old during this time of my life. I have already seen more that I should and been part of things that should never have happened, but I will save that personal information for another time and maybe another book! Anyhow, Janet would lay there on the floor for a while, then wake up, and act like absolutely zero had happened. By this time, I would have departed from this place and headed to a friend's house. This is where I would act absolutely like not a thing has happened. I was good that way!

I had bought a change of clothes and intended on spending the night. This family was mostly likely as normal as can be. What did this mean? No hand-to-hand combat while rolling on the floor with sharp knives. I was relieved and wore out from this night that didn't want to end.

After finally getting to sleep the phone started to ring at my friend's house around 3 AM. Since I was half asleep, I didn't hear the phone being picked up or the conversation. And then the door opened, and a voice said it's for you! All I could think was, what now? I picked up the phone and said hello, it was my father, who said, "Please come home!"

THE FACE THAT HAUNTED!

What did I do? Got up, got dressed, and proceeded to drive towards the island. All along with the thought of "What am I going to walk into?" As I reached the end of our driveway, I noticed that daddy's interior car lights were on, and his front doors were wide open. As I got closer, I then noticed all the lights were on at the house.

When I reached the front doorsteps, daddy met me at the door. And he had a look on his face that was strange enough. Daddy had deep scratches on his face and his white T-shirt was soaked in blood. And then he said, "Judy, Janet looks very bad, and I don't know what to do!"

My father had a strange way of turning everything around, then having me agree with him, and condoning what he had done. As a child and now as a young adult I labeled myself as "the watcher!" He always wanted me to watch when the beatings began and if I wasn't around, he made sure I was going to know exactly why it all happened.

Normally, according to him, she deserved it, and most of his wives/girlfriends did not fight back. It was then what I would come to call, a simple one-sided massacre. However, when it came to Janet, she fought back, bringing on the worst kind of ending!

When I walked into daddy's bedroom, the face that I would see would be one that I would have trouble forgetting. Although Janet was awake, her face was bruised, cut, eyes swollen, head wounded, and I could go on, but I really needed to look away.

I immediately told my father that Janet needed to go to the hospital. He told me he would take care of it, which meant we are going to deal with this right here!

I retreated to my room but could not get Janet's face out of my mind. And this wouldn't be the last time I would see Janet's face. It showed up in my dreams or should I say nightmares and in the most unlikely places. I remember this one time, while water skiing, that I had fallen, and while waiting for the boat to pick me up I thought I saw Janet's cut-up face right under the surface of the water. This so freaked me out that I stopped training and just went back to the dock.

Back to my Father's Open Casket Viewing...

On the night of my father's viewing, I walked down to the dock just to check out to the boats. And I noticed, being a person of the sea, and could feel a big weather change was on the horizon. With everything going on I didn't think much of it, and I didn't watch the evening weather news either.

When we arrived at the Fox and Weeks Funeral Home, which was located on Drayton Street, I was met by a couple of directors. When the funeral directors picked my father up at the nursing home, they told me that most likely it would have to be a closed casket. I was disappointed because, at least in my case, I always preferred an open casket! And we would take pictures too! Some people find this act of taking pictures morbid! In my case, if you have passed, I would like to see this for sure. I know this sounds crazy, but it is just the way I was raised.

The best news was that the mortician was able to make my father presentable and I would be having, as requested, an open casket viewing! I know most people would not smile about this, but I did. The directors told me that I could have some time alone with my father and that made me happy too!

Captain Sherman I. Helmey 1902-1993!

34

DADDY IN THE CASKET!

As you can see, we had an open casket after all. And even though my father isn't with us any longer he still looked a lot better than he did before the funeral home did what they did! So, I thanked them very much! My father had lots of mourners at his wake. The fact of the matter is since he had been sick for about 5 years, I was certainly shocked at all the people! I was happy and sad at the same time.

While all the visiting and condolencing was taking place I was only half present. My other half was wondering who was buried next to my mother at the Helmey Grave site. Heck, tomorrow was the funeral and unless changes were made my father could not be buried!

Little did I know, but Mr. Johnson had told the office of his findings and then they planned to find out who was in the so-called wooden casket. So, being I wasn't involved, I didn't know what was going on. However, I still had to wonder if my father had allowed them to bury Janet at the Helmey burial site.

"Modified Bricks!"

This is a great story and one that my father didn't share with anyone. However, at my father's wake, (funeral) an older gentlemen told me this story. And I believe, if not mistaken, it was Mr. Byrd, owner, operator, and driver of Byrd Cookie Company for many years! And you have got to love a good story, and this is one of those that would have been lost forever, if Mr. Byrd had not remembered and shared with me! According to Mr. Byrd....

Way back in the good old days and before he started his career into the fishing world my father was known as "Great Mechanic." In the old days you just didn't plug a car into the old computer to ascertain what the problem was. You had to first find the problem and then figure out how to fix it. Not only that, but most parts were never in stock, or they might not have been invented yet. No matter what, there was usually something to order. This situation could add weeks, which could turn into many months before you could get your car fixed. My father according to sources was the man that could take weeks or maybe months out of your car or truck repair time.

Back in the thirties, my father's car/truck repair service was big, and he handled most of the delivery trucks in the Savannah area. And this is about where Mr. Byrd's story starts!

When drivers were having trouble, they would just stop Daddy's Garage to either drop the truck off or to talk about their trucking woes. This one driver stopped by to complain that his truck would not idle on its own. His problem was that when he stopped to make a quick delivery his truck would not idle on its own. It would always be stalling out on him. Back in the old days, batteries were not made for "continues cranking." In fact, if the trucks or cars just started on the first try in the morning it was said to be a genuine miracle.

My father asked, "Are you leaving your truck with us?" The driver replied, "Yes, how long do you think it will take to fix it?"

My father scratched his head and said, "Come by after lunch." My father, as usual, would basically start his own personal ritual of checking the truck out.

After lunch the driver stopped by to check on his truck. My father quickly told him that it was ready and handed the driver part of a brick. The driver took it with a puzzled look. My father explained, "When you stop to make a delivery simply put this brick on your accelerator." The driver didn't think much about it as far as he was concerned his delivery troubles were over. Daddy was known for his unusual tactics when addressing mechanical problems that drivers had.

As I got this story straight from the driver's mouth I had to ask about that old brick. The brick wasn't whole but instead modified. He had simply whacked off a couple of inches off the brick's length. Daddy's reasoning for this was that no matter what part of the accelerator you set the brick on it would hold the truck at the correct idling RPM only. All I can say is that "Technology in the thirties when it came to fixing cars and trucks was to just use the knowledge you had acquired to make them work!"

As you have most likely figured out, the driver was Mr. Byrd himself! And just when you thought you heard it all another story surfaces! My father, no matter what, lived an interesting life!

This just looks like a random pile of discarded bricks. This couldn't be further from the truth. They could be used as parts, or they could be used as tools to fix certain broken complicated ways of this mechanical thing we call a car!

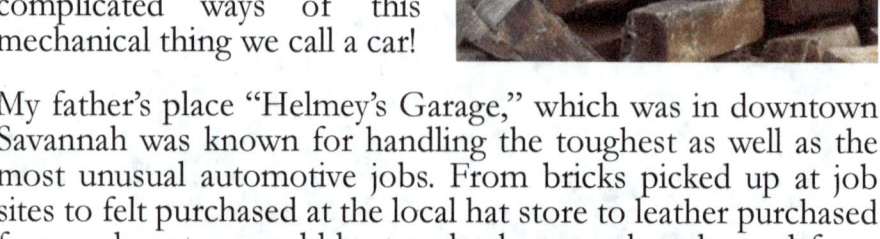

My father's place "Helmey's Garage," which was in downtown Savannah was known for handling the toughest as well as the most unusual automotive jobs. From bricks picked up at job sites to felt purchased at the local hat store to leather purchased from a downtown cobbler to who knows what else and from where!

JANET PETTENGILL'S MURDER...

Boy, I got to tell you this story about my father's funeral has a lot of turns and twists. So, I guess it is time to bring you up to speed on the evening that Janet's body had been found lying on the side of the road in Savannah's west side. It was late one night, the phone rang, daddy answered it, there was a long pause, and I heard him say, "I will be right down!" Then I heard daddy say, "Judy that was the police station and they want me to come down and identify a body, which they say might be Janet's!"

Since, we hadn't seen Janet for a while I stood straight up in bed. Daddy said, "Do you want to ride with me and wait in the car!" And I replied, "Yes!" As we made our way to the police station, which at the time was in downtown Savannah, we didn't say much! I was thinking what the heck and I can only assume that daddy was thinking about what he was just about to see.

I watched as daddy walked into the police station. Then all I could think of was I wonder how long this would take and I am glad I am not going in with him. After about an hour I watched as daddy came out of the station and headed to the car. According to my father the police officer took daddy directly back to the morgue. Once inside he basically showed daddy Janet. After looking at her charred body, hardly unrecognizable face, jewelry, half burn clothing, and what was left of the wig he finally remarked, "That's Janet!"

THE PETTENGILL BABY BOY!

Mr. Franks drove up ...(not his real name)

So, basically, after this time not much was ever said again about Janet. That is until about 17 years later and then this happened.

A car drove up in the yard, he got out and asked to speak to Captain Helmey. As always, I jokingly said, "Which one Daddy or me?"

His response was fast, he wanted to speak to my father! I replied, "give me a minute." I went inside and got daddy. He walked out and the gentleman introducing himself as Mr. Franks said, "Mr. Helmey I am here to talk with you about my adopted son!"

He is about 18 years old now and quite a problem. And I was wondering if I could bring him to your house to stay with you for a while. Maybe it would be a good thing for the boy, and I know it would be for us!"

I have covered the names of petitioners, (those adopting Pettengill baby) because the story is not about them. It is about Janet and all the things she did!

STATE OF SOUTH CAROLINA,

COUNTY OF __BEAUFORT__

PETITIONERS

PETTENGILL BABY, a minor,
JANET COWART PETTENGILL and
CHARLES EDWARD PETTENGILL

RESPONDENTS

SUMMONS & PETITION
(copy)

BROWN & BROWN
ATTORNEYS AT LAW
RIDGELAND, S. C.

ATTORNEYS FOR __Petitioners__

WALKER, EVANS & COGSWELL CO., CHARLESTON, S. C.   59084

(203)726-5593

THE ASK?

Well as you can imagine, that very long sentence that Mr. Franks just said caught my attention. I looked at my father, and he had a puzzling look on his face. According to Mr. Franks he had adopted a baby boy from Janet Pettengill and that my father had assisted monetarily somewhat over the years. And then he showed me a picture of his adopted son. I could not look away.

Mr. Franks asked if he could bring his son over the next day and my father said OK. As he drove down the driveway, I had to ask, "Daddy, what the heck is he talking about?" And since my father at this time was experiencing serious dementia, he really couldn't answer, because he had no past memory. So, all I could think was I am going to have to handle this somehow some way.

It was a long night, and I didn't sleep too well. Heck, after all I had a lot on my mind and mostly about the 17-year-old Pettengill Baby. The next day came quickly, and Mr. Franks drove up, but he was alone. He got out of the car and said that his son refused to come. And I didn't say anything because I didn't know what to say. And of course, my father wasn't saying anything. I thought the best thing to do was to let Mr. Frank's do all the talking. He said, "If it is OK, can I bring my son if he ever wants to come and meet you?" And I answered for daddy, who was a million miles away, of course. And I gave him a business card. And that is the last time I ever saw Mr. Franks or ever got close to getting an opportunity to meet my possible, but most likely ½ brother.

And the snow covered the ground and the winds did howl! So therefore, the actual burying of my father was delayed about 3 days!

THE DAY OF MY FATHER'S FUNERAL...

After my father's wake and right before I was supposed to bury him at the Helmey plot. The Storm of the Century hit the next morning bringing with it 80 mile-an-hour winds and snow-like conditions that the south had never seen before! Since dangerous weather conditions prevailed daddy's funeral was delayed for a couple of days. So, we waited until the weather cleared!

This is a picture taken right before I did what I did! Read on!

After the snow melted and the winds calmed, we had our grave side funeral for my father. The preacher read a wonderful poem about my father that Wil Denmark had written! All attendees were standing by the grave site watching as daddy's coffin was lowered into the concrete vault. As soon as the cover of the vault was situated, I said, "Stop!" And of course, everyone looked at me waiting for me to do whatever I was going to do. Well, I had a pint of liquor in my pocket that Wil had given me! I thought it would be appropriate for me (Captain Judy) to lay the bottle on top of the vault. However, to get to the vault, I had to step down into the grave. At this moment, I thought I could hear people gasping for air! Once I made my descend, I placed the bottom on top of the vault and then turned to say to those holding the shovels, "You had better not bother my

43

father liquor!" And they all answered in cadence, meaning they all shook their heads at the same time!

Since my father always said the best liquor is OP, which meant "Other Peoples!" I thought putting the liquor Wil brought would only be proper if I delivered it in pure Captain Judy style! I can only assume that this highlight for me for my father came under lots of family scrutiny. However, I bet that this action provided the family with a lot to talk about around the dinner table! Don't you just love a great story!

After 5 days of waiting for the weather to clear,
we finally laid Captain Sherman I. Helmey to rest!

The, Janet Called!

After what seemed like more than a full day of burying my father I arrived home and let out a big sigh of relief. I had just made me my favorite drink, which was during this time a Crown Royal over ice with a splash of Coke! As I was raising my glass for my first slip, the phone started ringing. Since all my friends had been answering the phone for the last few days, it was my turn! I picked up the phone and said, "Miss Judy Charters!" And voice on the other end said, "This is Janet I am sorry to hear about your father!" What did I reply? To be honest, I cannot remember!

I know I am jumping around, and I really can't help it for sure! When it came to Janet Pettengill there was a lot to write about. There were things that I found out after the fact and believe me there is more to come. So now we are going to forward past my father's funeral twenty some years ahead. Now let's talk about the so-called murder of Janet Pettengill...

The Murder Plot Thickens!

I guess you already know I was shocked and immediately wondered why she had stayed away and was just calling at this time! My father went to his grave thinking she was murdered in 1968! Not only that, but he had gone to the police station and identified her body. And if I had to guess, my father most likely had her buried on the family plot in the wooden coffee, which I wasn't aware of until I tried to bury him in 1993. And of course, as the years passed more information, through no fault of my own, about Janet just surfaced!

THEN THIS HAPPENED,
MY NEIGHBOR THE PRIEST IN 2009...

Then this happened, my neighbor the priest in 2009…

In 2009, in the Publix grocery store and I ran into a neighbor priest friend of mine. We were all raised at the same time and our families have been neighbors since 1951. As children we all played together! The priest told me that I had certainly did lead an interesting life! And he of course was right, thanks to dear old dad! Anyhow, the priest told me that he had this information about my stepmother's murder.

Bringing you up to speed and myself. He was talking about Daddy's so-called murdered wife Janet, who had his baby which was adopted by our relatives in South Carolina ...by this time I knew that the lady murdered was most likely Janet's roommate at the time. Since I had talked to Janet on the day of my father's funeral in 1993!

The detective friend told the Priest that he thought the lady murdered which they still thought was Janet Pettengill (my father's girlfriend/maybe wife) had been murdered/tortured by convicted serial killer Peewee Gaskins. Now, yet another twist to this ongoing story!

Meet Peewee Donals Henry Gaskins

The detective also said that the way Janet (supposedly had been murdered and tortured) had definite similarities to the way Peewee murdered/tortured his victims. And Peewee was here on a killing spree during this time...

Here's is where it gets interesting... The priest told me that the detective who was the one who interviewed the serial murderer Peewee Gaskins was with the Savannah Police department. The detective was friends with Wilbur Cubbage, another neighbor and father to Linda, Donna and Debra, they lived over on Dogwood Avenue). This detective owned a T-Craft shrimp boat named Rojo. The detective kept it tied up at the Police dock on Turner Creek. I know all this information seems like just word filler. However, it is not, since I am not using names, all those in the know, when and if they read this will understand!

The serial killer's name was Peewee Gaskins! He was interviewed by this detective when this beast was on death row in SC. He'd already been convicted of several killings. Peewee Gaskin, referred to the death of Janet as one of his many "Coastal Killings." Supposedly he would just have to kill someone every 6 weeks or so. He said that he'd torture them, make it last and do it slowly. This victim (supposedly Janet) was found on the side of a road on the west side of Savannah. Janet had her hands tied behind her back with her belt. She had been choked, stabbed and her throat was cut. Then she had been doused with a flammable liquid and set on fire.

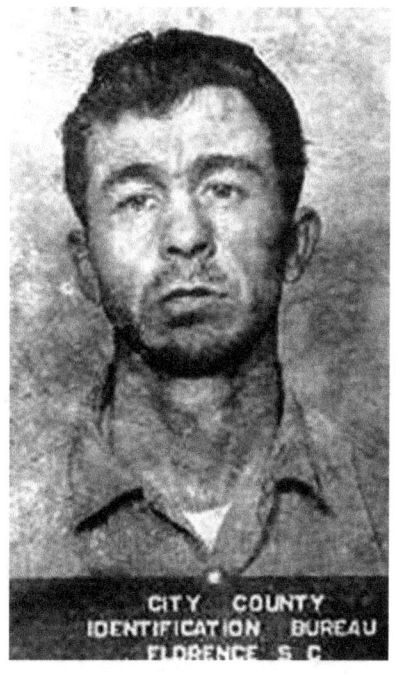

Peewee Gaskins

47

The detective said that Peewee was able to recall unbelievable details without any remorse or emotion. It was as if he was watching it on TV. Peewee would recall things like the smell of the match being lit, birds singing while she cried, and the feel of her belt in his hands. The detective said, "It was the closest to pure evil that he'd ever had the misfortune to encounter!"

It was a Closed Deal, or Was It?

The murderer revealed to the detective that in addition to the horrific things that she had already encountered, he'd shot her and tied a chain around her neck. These details were never made public. And so, it was because of this intimate knowledge of never unrevealed details in his confession that he deemed his information credible. And this is how this detective closed one of Savannah's more vicious murders.

Then after all the above took place...

More years later I finally got to look at some of the real information that was found in microfiche files. With the help of the Savannah Police Department Record Supervisor, I got a better idea of what exactly happened. The only way I could have pulled all these many years of information is to have lived it. If you are still reading at this point you now are in the know too! It has already been a crazy ride!

IN BLACK AND WHITE PRINT, IT STATED...

On September 26, 1968, the body was found on Kollock Street (west side of Savannah) on the side of the road. The body was laid face up and her assailant had tried to burn her on the spot. There was a wine color belt around her chin and some garments about her face. The belt around the face was a plastic type and there had been a belt around feet and ankles. There was a good imprint of a burned belt between her feet and the belt buckled on the east side of her right foot, which belonged to the belt that had been around her feet.

The body was still clothed in panties, bra, and some garments above the breast that were blood soaked, and which had not been completely burnt. On the right ring finger was a gold ring set with blue star sapphire set with 2 small diamonds. (one on each side)

As I looked through all the paperwork I received and I also found that the body had short jet-black hair! And there were remnants of a possible wig left and missing upper dentures.

JANET'S HAIR, HER WIG,
HER BELT, AND HER JEWELRY...

Why did my father think that the body he was looking at was Janet? Believe me that everything that you have read in the last two paragraphs screams Janet. He recognized her hair, the belt, the wig, her dentures missing, underwear, and jewelry. And now I believe after reading all that I have that this woman was wearing Janet's stuff, because she might have been a roommate. I don't have to tell you that roommates share things.

Janet's apartment address was number 8 Drayton Street and when the detective finally got inside there seem to be plenty incriminating evidence. All the lights were on and the faucet in the bathroom was wide open running. There were washed clothes hanging, two suitcases full of men's clothing, and a man shaving kit.

There was an assortment of blood accumulations along with a lady's white uniform. The uniform had blood stains located in about the same place the body did meaning she might have had it on at one time of the assault.

The ladies in Apartment 7 Drayon Street names were Mabel Rogers and Joan McCumber both told the detectives that Janet and Edward had left to go on vacation to New Orleans. And they were talking about Janet Pettengill and Edward Lane. They also told the detectives that it would be sometimes in October before the couple would return!

The Savannah detective contacted the New Orleans Police Department and had the couple picked up, just for identification purposes. At least that is what I read in the police paperwork. So, I can only guess that this couple never returned to Savannah! And they were never questioned about this murder. Or at least there is no paperwork to back this up. Now how crazy is this?

From what I recall, the unfortunate possible victim was a dancer at The Club Cebue? This strip club was in downtown Savannah on East Broughton near Price Street. And BINGO, she was also Janet Pettengill's roommate!

It is still somewhat of a cold case! At least in my eyes! This was a puzzle that I almost completely put together. However, there are still some questions that I have, but I am going to put them on the wayside for another time! It is official we are now moving on!

OGLETHORPE HOTEL POOL!

Although this is not a great picture, in the black/white taking photos days, you had to take what you could get. This is me posing at the Oglethorpe Hotel pool. My mother and I used to go there all the time! And I loved jumping off the high dive!

I found this old postcard! This was the 1930's version on the Oglethorpe Hotel located on Wilmington Island Road, Savannah, Georgia!

SAND PITS!

This hotel has so much history that if I started writing about what I think I know we would be here for a while. Here is what I would like to share with you. My father used to say, "In Las Vegas the mafia buried their dead in the desert. On Wilmington Island they buried their dead on the Oglethorpe Hotel golf course in the sand pits!"

According to my father digging in the sand was easier and better than disturbing the greens. And my father also said, "Parts of Jimmy Hoffa were buried under the helicopter pad at the hotel.

Then there is another rumor that parts of Hoffa are also buried on the 18 the hole at the Oglethorpe. Rumor had it they those who knew of Hoffa whereabouts peed on this area before moving on! According to my father this wasn't considered a burial, it was a statement!

As you know, my father worked with the well-known Al Capone gangster association in the 1930's. Since I wasn't born until 1951, I really don't know for a fact.

However, here's what I do know…my father certainly did know a lot about all the goings on. When he talked about it his eyes would light up and that big cigar that he was smoking produced some of the thickest smoke rings around his head that I have ever seen. And this was his sign that big conversations were going on!!

My standard line for those that read this stuff is this: This information must be true because I'm certainly not smart enough to make it up!

PUTTING EASTER BACK ON TRACK!

On every Easter morning I knew the Easter Bunny most likely had come to visit, but when he didn't… If my father forgot to put the Easter Bunny's baskets out, he would always say, "The Easter Bunny's truck broke down! At six years old, since we had so many cars and trucks, I understood mechanical difficulties. (Even if I couldn't pronounce it!) Heck, this sort of thing happened all the time and daddy was always working on one of them! Then he would say, "He called me last night and I had to go pick up your Easter surprises! I left everything on the backseat of my car!" Putting Easter back on track!

I had a wonderful childhood and the older I get the more I appreciate it! My father left me a lot of wonderful things to write about!

My mother dressed me for Easter Day Success! I am wearing white patent-leather shoes instead of my signature black!

The Easter Bunny Has Arrived!

Even at the request of the Easter Bunny never hide the Easter baskets in the trunk of your car and here's why!

My father always had a lot of good stuff in the trunk of his car. We never had a truck to throw things in, so daddy's car trunk, to say the least, was always full of something. One afternoon right before Easter, I was in the front seat of the car and daddy said, "I have to get something out of the trunk!"

While he jumped out, I turned around in the seat and watched his every move. He was funny sometimes the way he would fling his arms. I watched as he opened the trunk and through the crack in the lid, I could see most of what daddy was doing. To the right of the trunk were all sorts of things sticking up and then it caught my eye. There was something covered in red tinted cellophane. As I looked even closer it occurred to me that I had seen this sort of packaging before.

This photo was taken in our kitchen back in the mid-fifties by the Mr. Easter Bunny! The middle Easter basket was the one that was allegedly crushed in the car trunk!

55

Just as my small mind started to wonder I watched daddy pull something from the trunk while slamming the trunk at about the same time. The red cellophane package got crushed in the process. I heard a loud cracking noise and watched as daddy struggled with the lock that opened the trunk. After a few seconds I got tired of watching and turned away to play with knobs on the radio. On Easter Sunday morning I jumped out of bed and ran into the kitchen with hopes of an Easter Bunny surprise. As I rounded the corner into the kitchen right there on the kitchen chairs was not one Easter basket, but three. And I might add that even though the basket in the middle was a little crushed with a few damaged toys I still ruled when it came to having the most baskets delivered at one time by the Good Old Easter Bunny!!

This is me around 4 years old, holding a rabbit that Daddy did not shoot. I must have loved my black Patent leather shoes; because I have seen several pictures with what looks like these same pair of shoes. Or maybe my father who was notorious for purchasing things by the dozens had most likely purchased many pairs!"

Here's what I remember about Easter and my daddy…

Patent Leather shoes were a must no matter what you wore with them with!

Oglethorpe Hotel has great Easter Egg Hunts!

For those looking for a great place to hide that golden egg for the Easter egg hunt here's a suggestion

Place the golden egg in the gutter (where the water flows out) and then push a hand full of moss in the pipe to keep it there. Let some of the moss hang out as if it is hung in the gutter. Just so you will know when the moss is pulled out the golden egg rolls right out with it. How do I know this…When I was six years old, I saw, as well as another golden egg searcher, the moss hanging out of the gutter. While we both started making our way to this spot we collided. After running right into each other we both fell and the contents of our Easter egg baskets went everywhere. We both watched as another pulled the moss and rolled out the golden egg. Moral of the golden egg story is a simple one…

Before looking for the whereabouts of the golden egg whatever you do, "Always be prepared!" Have your father put scrapes on the bottom of your new patent leather shoes, put your basket down first, and then run faster than the others with the same goal!

For those that don't know, laying scrapes on the bottom of your patent leather shoes causes much needed traction especially when dealing with slippery wet grass! I must ask, "Where did my father come up with all these things?"

THE CURSE DELIVERED!

The Ladies that visited Oglethorpe Hotel later known as the Savannah Inn and Country Club.

In the thirties, forties, fifties, and sixties there was this thing that was taken care of. Back in the war days there was the USO. Well, on Wilmington Island where the Oglethorpe Hotel was located all sorts of ladies were invited to visit and possibly stay!

These were not ladies of the evening nor were they working girls they were ladies that came to spend time with the gentlemen that were staying at the hotel. The fact of the matter is according to some there was pay involved for this type of let's say, "Clean entertainment!" And there were some that were exactly what you think they were. My aunt called them "Peacocks!" I will let you let your mind take you wherever you want to go with that information!

So now that I have rambled enough, I will get to the story that I was told that prompted this interesting tale. There was this painting of 3 or maybe 4 ladies that hung in the hotel lobby for many years. These ladies were all smiling and dressed to the Nines!

For those not familiar with the term "Dressed to the Nines?" I will try to explain. This term is used to describe a lady's attire, in this case, in which it is either very flamboyant or considered smartly dressed. It has been said and noticed by many in the know that when it comes to different types of attire gentlemen tend to have different tastes.

The ladies in the picture were all dressed differently while sporting big smiles! I don't know when the first call was made or when this so-called dilemma started.

Sometimes in the sixties a call was made to the lobby desk. It was a lady who claimed that she was one of the ladies in the painting that was hanging on the wall across from the hotel lobby desk. She said, "Whoever removes this picture will not live to see the sunrise on the next day!" And of course, no names were given, and the phone quickly went dead.

The unfortunate person that answered the phone although baffled didn't say anything to anyone, at least maybe not right away! After taking a good look at the painting she realized where it hung had in fact been painted around not behind. The painting was not moved and after a better observation you could see that they were several different colors of wall paint that had been traced around the outside of the frame.

Leaving nothing to chance...

I don't want to leave nothing to chance when it comes to this story. As a reader you need the facts and I as the writer am going to try to give them to you. This tale is kind of like those Terminator movies that start in the middle of the story! So therefore, the next movie installments are either forward or backward in time. They leave you with a big question mark in mind until the next movie is released.

Since the painting that my father told me about is no longer hanging on the wall in the Lobby at the Oglethorpe Hotel aka Savannah Inn and no one seems to know what I am talking about here are my theories:

Let's say for the story's sake that the last call was made in the sixties, which means the lady in the lobby did not pass on the proposed curse. She did or did not remove the painting nor was the information passed on. My question …did she live to see sunrise the next day?

So, since my father was the one that told me about this story apparently it was one that passed around for many years. After all the painting was still hanging in the lobby in the sixties! According to the story, the painting was painted around and not under until the sixties. So therefore, a call by the lady in the picture must have been made earlier in time.

Let's say for argument's sake that the lady in the picture called every year so that her curse lived on. Apparently, those at the lobby desk receiving the calls for all those years must have shared it. Let's face it, if this information was shared then everyone knew about it. And no one would dare ever remove the painting. It had to be shared with the maintenance workers, because how would they have known not to remove but paint around it! Superstitions back in the old days ran rampant! And then there were those that weren't superstition at all! However, with this said information onboard they still would have most likely not moved the painting.

So therefore, now that you have read this story, if you or you knew someone that worked at Oglethorpe Hotel or Savannah Inn during these times that has possibly heard such a story or got a call at the front hotel desk, please by all means contact me with the details 912 897 4921.

And for those of you that did get the call and didn't move the picture, but don't want to talk about it I understand! For those that got the call, but still moved by the picture, I must wonder about whether you got to see that sunrise or not! It is a simple question!

Now unfortunately, this is not the picture of the ladies that I am writing about. However, since I never was personally introduced to any of the ladies, it just might be one of them!

Is This Lady Standing By Alone?

I have some updated information on this picture, which I received from a reader. I published "The Ladies that visited Oglethorpe Hotel later known as the Savannah Inn!"

The picture shown below with the man silhouetted behind the lady was not always seen. According to my source, who worked for many years at this hotel, was very familiar with this picture. Not only was he very familiar so were the people that chose to check it out continuously. Why? Sometimes the man in the background would be there as plain as day. And then there were times no matter how you approached or stared at the picture the only thing you would see was the Lady in the light green dress!

Update... The artist was asked why she didn't paint in a gentlemen in on both ladies...and her reply was simple... I didn't add a gentlemen to either painting!

New Year's Eve
at the Grand Oglethorpe Hotel

I must admit that this is one of those stories that I wrote and every time I re-read it, I re-live it! I am so happy that my memory banks are still intact.

Photos by Jerry Helmey (my mother)

Yes, this is me sitting on the stern of Daddy's wooden boat "Miss Jerry." My mother most likely was taking the picture, because daddy would never have thought of putting the hotel in the background. As you can see it pretty much looks the same way today as it sits on beautiful Wilmington River. However, unfortunately it's no longer known as the Grand Oglethorpe Hotel! However, for me it will never be anything else!

My father used to go to their New Year Eve Party every year. And to get the story started I must state my grandmother lived and worked at the hotel. So therefore, he could drop me off and then walk right into the main lobby of the hotel and right into the famous Emerald Room. This was the hotel's ballroom, which was unbelievable to a 7-year-old. I really don't know where to start regarding this story, because there is so much to write.

This is a picture of my mother (Jerry) my father (Captain Sherman Helmey) and My grandmother. I called her Mommie Leech! And you must recognize me, little Captain Judy, who is much too busy to look at the camera!

My Grandmother

Firstly, let's get this part of the story out of the way. My grandmother on my mother's side worked at the hotel in linen services. I guess that's what it's called. She worked down under the hotel taking care of making sure all the linens were washed and pressed properly. Yes, I said, "Pressed properly!" The linens were ironed back then for the hotel beds. And each bed had to be made up in a certain way, but to this day I never understand why. All I know is I couldn't help doing this part. However, I could fluff the pillows, which was always my job. My grandmothers' room looked like a hotel room. It didn't have a kitchen because all meals were picked up at the hotel's kitchen. I can't remember whether I liked the food or not. However, what I do remember is individual pats of butter, small helpings of all types of jellies, and everything on a separate covered plate. All plates, coffee cups, and tea glasses set on what my grandmother called a "dolly." We basically had the time of our lives picking up the food, coming back to the room, and eating off a tray. It was great!

At the age of seven I wasn't allowed to roam around much, but when I was, I made tracks. I found out quickly that from the linens services you could get almost anywhere. It was an adventure from the word go. Once everyone met me my travels broadened. I could run to the kitchen grab a piece of toast; butter it up with an actual paint brush and get back to my mission.

The Toaster!

Before I go any further, I must tell you about this toaster. It reminded me of a sideways merry go around. The white bread was put on the rack and as it went up the burners inside were toasted on one side and as it came down the other side of the toast was cooked. It never stopped. As the toast came around it was taken off, buttered, cut in half, and put on a saucer. After a while I would just run up, pick out my piece of toast, paint it with butter and off I would go. Life was good, especially while eating on the run!

The Emerald Room!

I'll never forget the day I found the ballroom which was called the Emerald Room. It had dark green velvet curtains that seemed to go forever from the ceiling to the floor. It was a big room, and on this day, there were men with tall white hats chipping away at large chunks of ice. There was certainly a lot going on. The tables were being set with colorful party hats, horns, and swing around noisemakers. Not only was that, but lots of streamers of all colors were being draped from one end to another. Balloons were being tied everywhere; it was festive for sure! Being a child, my main goal was trying to get one of those noisemakers. Sure, enough, a nice gentleman also dressed in a tall white hat fixed me right up. I now had a hat, horn, and noisemaker. However, I was instructed not to blow the horn or swing the noisemaker in the hotel. I am sure glad he told me that because my plan was to parade through the Governor's Lounge and to see how much attention I could get.

Photo by Jerry Helmey

This is me once again trying to either hold up or just plain shoot at someone. I have always been fascinated with guns. In this case "cap guns." I must tell you while I am writing this, I can smell the smoke that a cap gun makes when fired. It's funny what you remember. As a child, during my cap gun phase I fired off roll after roll. I shot at everything from the trees to the ground. As you can see in this picture, I was dressed for cowboy success!

GOVERNOR'S LOUNGE

Since I mentioned it, I might as well tell you about the Governor's lounge. This room was situated on the ground level floor of the hotel. It had lots of windows so you could see outside while sitting down. They should have called it the Lounging room instead because there were chair and sofas all over the room. Heck, I could jump from one to another without even touching the floor. As a child I didn't understand what all the sitting was about. However, this room was sure was used a lot. It was always packed full of people drinking and smoking big cigars. As far as watching, this was the easiest room to get to. You could just walk in from outside, shoot right behind the sofas, and never be seen. I ought to know, I made a lot of strategic moves in this place working my way through all the furniture.

BEAUTIFUL ICE SWANS

Apparently, the day that I received the party favors must have been New Years Eve. I remembered daddy had dropped me off earlier that morning and said he wouldn't see me till tomorrow. Believe me, there was no crying here. Don't get me wrong. I love my father, but just thinking about running around the hotel was pretty darn exciting. After all I had to make the best out of what I was handed. My daddy used to say just like brier rabbit did "Please don't throw me in briar patch!" Well in this case, I was like that old rabbit; I wanted to stay at the hotel.

Since I couldn't really do much with my party favors, I decided to take them back to my grandmother for safekeeping. As soon as I dropped my goods off, I headed back to the Emerald Room, because I wanted to see what those big blocks of ice looked like now. To my amazement they had carved two ice swans, which pretty much mesmerized me!

The next day my father picked me up. When we got into the car on the seat was a party hat, horn, and a swinging noisemaker. I was surprised when he handed them to me and when he told me about the swans that were made from ice. As I listened to him talk about things that I already knew I was happy to know that he had not missed out on anything either!

It is all about Wilmington Island and Oglethorpe Hotel aka Savannah Inn and Country Club!

This is one of the most beautiful colorful pictures of the Savannah Inn taken by Bill Vanderford! The Barbara Negra moored to the right was at its all time glory!

Once again, for us elders, it is called and always will be "The Old Oglethorpe Hotel!"

BILL VANDERFORD

My very good friend for many years Bill Vanderford is a very successful writer, author of many books, racer car driver, fisherman, photographer, fishing guide, traveler, and I think you get the point. My friend has conquered many quests in high style. Way back when I first started getting serious about charter fishing, not just my life, but my career I was lucky to have met Bill.

When I first met Bill, we hit is off right away. It has always been said, especially in the good old days when newspapers and magazines were king, that if you had a true sport writer on your side as your friend, they could help your cause! And that is true for a fact, and I had one of the biggest, and his name was Bill Vanderford! When my charter fishing business slowed, I would call Bill, tell him the situation, and he would always take care of it. You see, Bill Vanderford's articles were so popular that when they hit the newsstands people who read them started making some definite southern tracks.

Bill took some fabulous pictures of our area, which he always shared with me! And now you get to see them too!

I can't thank him enough! And Bill is still doing successfully what he has been doing for many years, which is talking fishing, writing superb articles, taking great pictures, and making the Atlanta highways his current speedway! A big thanks from Captain Judy!

Bill Vanderford

70

BARBA NEGA SAILING VESSEL!

Looks like a serious pirate vessel and acts like one too! The Babra Negra was built in 1896! She was a 121-foot fishing Ketch, vintage 1896 Norwegian Barquentine.

Everyone loves a great pirate, the stories they tell, and the talking parrot that backs them up!

The Barba Nega, photo by Bill Vanderford

The first time that I ever met Gerhard Schwisow was at my house, which is located on Wilmington Island. As well as I can remember it was during the late seventies. I always knew him as Gary, but as it turns out his first name was Gerhard. At any rate

Gerhard Schwisow 1947-2006

he had stopped by to ask my father, Captain Sherman Helmey, if he could charter his boat Miss Jerry for a film expedition. As he talked it came to light that Gerhard needed to rent several crews carrying charter boats. It was a large camera crew because multiple angles had to be shot at the same time. This is just about when the evening drinks started along with big stories of catching fish and other things. It seemed it didn't take too long before my father and Gerhard found out that they had something in common and it wasn't the sea alone.

As I stood there and listened it all sounded so exciting. I had seen when Gerhard had sailed what was called the tall ship "Barba Negra" in from the ocean. As she made her way up the Wilmington River more and more boats took to following this pirate-looking sailing vessel. It soon came to rest at the Savannah Inn Sheraton dock. It looked like a real-life pirate ship with all the trimmings of cannons, galley's, many tall masts to swing from, and even a live talking parrot. I must add that this parrot had quite a vocabulary with a pirate accent.

As Gerhard and my father talked, they found that they both had interest in boats and women. My father at the time had been married at least 7 times and had never stopped dating. Little did we know number eight was just around the corner! Gerhard was a handsome man, tan, and had an accent. Back in those days I called it his "lure tone" of sorts! Good-looking women must have just loved to hear him talk, because there were always plenty around to listen.

Daddy, Gerhard, and I talked about many things over the years, but the one thing that amazed me most with his expertise in the boat-repairing department. He took a ship that was being eaten up by worms that in most cases you couldn't even see and fix it. As I remember this was the first time, I had ever seen a boat with a total copper bottom. My father's boat had what I call "copper patches."

The "Barba Negra" had a total covered copper bottom. It was truly an amazing accomplishment. All I could think about when looking at it was how the heck did, they got a piece of copper that big in the first place? I never asked so I never knew. I'm sure it took hundreds of screws, bolts, and tacks to hold it to the ship's hull. The good news was that his theory worked, she floated high taking on just the right amount of water.

I came home one day from fishing and noticed that Gerhard had a large clear plastic tent that covered almost the entire out of water part of the ship. I had to hear this story. So therefore, as soon as I cleaned my boat up, I stopped by. According to

Gerhard worms were now eating at a good part of the upper half and the main mast of the ship. To kill the wood boring vermin a special exterminator was hired to fumigate the tented area. These worms had been dormant for the longest time. For some reason the colony of worms had become active and hungry. I didn't tell anyone, but I often wonder if it was that loud talking parrot that woke the mess of them up in the first place!

The bottom line of the story is that Gerhard Schwisow was an extraordinary person, very nice looking in a pirate way, and a very likable person. I know that he will be missed by many and forgotten by none! I wish to send my sincere condolences to the family and friends of our fine sailing friend.

I do not know where the picture came from. I think it was taken from Daddy's boat "Miss Jerry" while they were filming the pirate movie. The Barba Nega was in full sail! The picture was taken in Wassaw Sound. In the background is green maker 19 to the right of the ship. In the background is Wassaw Island. And I'm sure that Gary is on board with lots of lady pirates and that talking parrot!

This is the pirate ship Barba Nega, which was tied up that the Savannah Inn's dock, which was located on the Wilmington River! This hotel is better known by us elders as the old Oglethorpe Hotel. Photo by Bill Vanderford

A beautiful sunset in the west on the Wilmington River located Savannah, Georgia! Bill captured the prefect sun set as it dropped behind Modena Planation! These were the good old times!

HAHN'S BEDROOM WINDOW STORY!

Now you must be thinking, why would I take a picture of this window?
Well, there is a story worth telling and this window is part of it.
This picture could also be considered one worth almost a thousand words!
Photo by Captain Judy.

The bedroom window that had to open before a move could be made!

This is my long-time neighbor's window. Now as far as names are concerned I am certainly not going to mention any complete names. As you know my father was a "rounder," which means he went out a lot and didn't care much about what others thought. However, when he found out someone was talking about him, he basically liked it, because this is how a "card" thinks. In my father's case, according to him the more they talked the easier it was to confront his so-called enemies. I know I shouldn't say, "enemies," because you certainly wouldn't want to label them that. So, we will call them what my father called them "The Busy Body Brigade!" This just means these are people who were bored with their own lives and loved to talk about my father's. Believe me, there was a lot to talk about when it came to my father truly colorful life escapades.

According to my father, most of the time it was someone's lonely wife that had the most to say. In my father's case he always thought they had some sort of crush on him. According to my father all women loved him! As a child I watched as women did fall all over him and in most cases, he wasn't really interested unless they had certain qualities. My father used to say, "Some women remind him of one of those water beads that quickly rolls off of a duck's back." Meaning only here for a very short visit! My father really did have some interesting sayings, and, in most cases, I understood, but can't explain why!

I know I need to get back to the window picture. This house was located at the front of our driveway. While looking through this window you could easily see my father's coming and goings even if it was in the early morning hours. According to daddy if you waited up for this event it was for some serious thoughts for sure. At any rate, once daddy got wind of all the scuttlebutt, he decided to make his going and coming a real interesting event. The first thing he did was to start by stopping at the window and blowing the car's horn until someone either came out or opened the window. He decided to break the one doing all the talking slowly, which means the first stops at the window were during the daylight hours. As time went on the stops got later and then they got earlier in the morning, meaning after daddy's evening had ended.

Many years ago, after my father had already gone to that big fishing ocean in the sky, I had a conversation with the husband of the wife who loved to talk about daddy. Since I didn't know anything about all of this, I was all-ears. It went something like this: According to the husband, "When your father started doing this in the middle of the day it wasn't so bad. The fact of the matter is I laughed." However, when it went from daytime to early mornings, I just wanted my wife to hurry up, open the window, scream "yes I know you are home Sherman!" According to the husband until his wife opened the window your father just kept blowing the horn! I will admit this; my father certainly did have loud car horns and in some case sirens too!

This is the first Miss Judy fiberglass boat, which was a Leslie Craft. This boat cruised at around 40 knots!

Coast guard operator asked, "Are you in imminent danger?"

DADDY COMMANDEERING
THE 4141 COAST GUARD CUTTER!

During the Early Seventies my father brought me a 28-foot Leslie Craft fiberglass boat. She was a used boat, but after Daddy worked on it for a while all was good. This boat of course was called Miss Judy, and she was a fast one for sure. And when I was running, believe me, I was going fast! At this time my father's wooden boat Miss Jerry was still docked at Captain Walsh's marina on Lazaretto Creek, Tybee Island. His boat's top speed underway was about 12 knots. So therefore, being tied up at Captain Walsh's dock meant a shorter ride to the fish. In my case, if I left Captain Walsh's dock, I would be fishing for a good 30 minutes before daddy arrived at the Black Fish Bank, which was located about 10 miles off Tybee Island.

On this fish day, I departed with my charter customers from Captain Walsh's dock. At the end of the fish day, I dropped my customers off, and my plan was to take my boat to our place located on Turner's Creek. The ride wasn't that long, especially in a boat that cruised at around 35 knots. Since tides were extremely low on this afternoon, I decided that skirting the large sand bars that were in the South Channel was not a very good idea. My plan was to go home by entering the Savannah River Shipping Channel. This meant I had to head a little offshore to get into the channel. As I made my turn into the mouth of the Savannah River it put incoming ships and calm ocean conditions to my stern. With my elbow propped on the windshield and with my long blonde hair blowing in the wind I was styling! As I was cruising around at about 38 knots without care in the world my engine just shut down. I jumped up, pulled the engine cover back, and took a good look into the hole. Absolutely not a thing jumped out at me meaning I wasn't on fire and my boat didn't seem to be taking on water. So here I was just floating with the incoming tide while making way at least 2 knots. Even in the seventies current in the Savannah was strong.

It wasn't dark time yet, but that situation wasn't far off. So, I decided to anchor as close as I could by the riverbank. However, this proved to be a little hard taking into consideration that I had no sort of power to push me there. So, I dropped the anchor and once it grabbed hold, I found myself in a pretty bad situation. I was basically anchored, not in the exact middle, but right on the edge of the deepest part of the ship's channel. The meant when a ship came into the river if it didn't see me, I was going to be basically rammed and most likely never heard of again!

With darkness upon me I turned my anchor light and picked up my marine radio since cell phones had not been invented yet! I hailed the Tybee Island Coast Guard Station on channel 16 and they answered me right away. I explained my situation in somewhat of a professional manner. The main concern from them was this, "Was I in imminent danger?" And of course, since I was not in imminent danger, at least for the moment or until a ship headed my way, I answered "negative!" I then asked, would they mind calling my father? After a few other non-important questions, they said they would call him. I gave them the same phone number that we have now, which was 912 897 2478. And then I gave them my father's name, Captain Sherman I. Helmey. It seemed that I could hear them writing all this information down. After this brief encounter with the coast guard on the marine radio it got quieter and darker by the minute.

So, I waited and after a couple of hours passed a call came over the radio hailing "Miss Judy!" I grabbed the mic, and answered, this is "Miss Judy," and closed with "over!" They answered by saying that they had contacted my father, and I was to standby on this channel, which I replied, "Miss Judy over and standing by." And that is all that they said!

Little did I know back at the Tybee Island Coast Guard Station phone conversations were getting a little heated! When they called my father, they told him I had broken down, was anchored in the Savannah River, and that I was not in any imminent danger. According to both sides of the story, of which I am sorry that I can't convey, because of the off-color language that may or may not have been used. According to the story, at this point, my father did all the talking after he heard them say that I was "not in any imminent danger." He asked one question, "Are you going to go and get her?" And the answer was, "No she is not in any imminent danger!" At this time, I was told that Daddy hung up on the coast guard.

This is the first Miss Judy fiberglass boat, which was a Leslie Craft. This boat cruised at around 40 knots!

At this time my father got in his car and drove or raced down to the Tybee Island coast guard station. At this time, once arriving to the coast guard dock, which was located on Lazaretto Creek, he told the young coast guard man that they were in fact going to get his daughter. As he was saying this, he was boarding the coast guard cutter, which I believe was the 4141. Daddy asked the young man did he know how to drive the boat, and he replied to no. It was at that time that daddy cranked the 4141 up and asked, "you are going or not?" The young coast guard man jumped on board while daddy also known as Captain Sherman I. Helmey took the helm.

Back at Miss Judy I sat in complete darkness watching for navigation lights coming from either direction of the river. After about three hours I saw in the distance a small dim light, which did not look like it was coming from a ship. As it got closer, my radio sounded off and it was the best sound ever, it was my father hailing me from the boat that was approaching! As soon as daddy aka 4141 got to my boat, he handed the helm over the young coastie. As the boat turned around, putting its stern at my bow, I watched as my father pick up a perfectly coiled rope and then handed it over to me. It didn't take but a few moments for me to get my anchored pulled and for them to get me under tow. As I was being towed by the 4141, I watched as my father sat on the stern waving at me while he held up a fifth of Canadian Mist in his other hand! And I remember this just as if it were only yesterday!!

I know this story sounds like it couldn't possibly be true. But... My father did in fact commandeer the coast guard cutter 4141 rescuing me, because according to him I was in fact in imminent danger! When all was said and done, I ended up meeting the poor unfortunate coast guard man that just happened to be on the boat dock when my father arrived. And his story was a simple one, He said, "It was the most exciting night that he had ever had while on watch at the coast guard station!" And then he added I certainly did learn a few things for sure! He also said, "That my father was indeed something else!"

I just hope that through my stories that I have brought to light that my father was truly a coastal colorful character in every way possible! And I wish I could have introduced him to everyone because he really was something else!

Mrs. Sanders Of Wilmington Island Story!

This is such a wonderful old story that I am going to have to scratch my head and shake it to remember all the details.

When I was very young, under the age of 10, I used to attend Sunday school classes on a regular basics. I enjoyed the company and watching all the wonderful people that I would get to see while attending church. It seemed that they were always dressed in their finest clothes, some even wore big hats. I have always said, "that a person who wears a hat knows exactly who they are and aren't afraid to show it!" It's true that all can wear hats; it's just how we wear them that makes them work. At any rate, there was this one beautiful lady that always attended church. She was always dressed to the "nines!" I really don't know where that terminology came from. It means she always looked great, and everything matched. Her outfits were unbelievable. She was one of those ladies that knew how to wear a big hat along with a veil of sorts. Her name was Mrs. Sanders. I was mesmerized by her. She was beautiful, was always very nice, and I quite often sat behind her in church.

At any rate Mrs. Sanders always came to church looking her absolute best. My favorite outfit was the one where she wore those foxes that bit each other on the tail. As a child I thought this was the most amazing thing to see. She wore four foxes that were held together with them biting each other's tail. For those that don't have a clue what I am talking about please pull this picture up in your mind.

Imagine that you have 4 foxes that are in full tact. This means they still have a head with real life-like features such as eyes, mouth, teeth, ears along with a body supporting four feet and a tail. They reminded me of the foxes that you always saw being chased by the hunters on horses. Take your fox's laid them out head to tail. Now attach the head of the fox to the tail in front of him. After attaching your four foxes you now have a line of foxes. Throw this around your shoulder and you then have

81

foxes seemly running around your neck while biting each other on the tail. As a child it was a confusing thing, but after I knew they weren't real or should I say, "still alive" it worked for me. I must say one more thing about the foxes, they were alive at one time. Mrs. Sanders must have loved them because it was one of her favorite wintertime coats. We saw foxes a lot during the cooler months. All the four fox heads had a different expression

frozen on their face. That's all I am going to say about this.

Mrs. Sanders had a couple of daughters, who were also very beautiful. However, I never saw any of them wearing a fox! I guess there was only one if those style coats in the family! Her daughters also dressed in very fashionable clothes! I always look forward to seeing them at church. Heck, it certainly made my day! I never remember seeing Mr. Sanders at church.

One day my father took me, and we went for a ride. Normally when we turned out of our driveway we always turned left, which was toward town. However, today daddy took a right turn on this day. It really didn't matter to me, because I really never knew where we were going anyway, at least until we arrived at our destination. Heck, sometimes we would end up in Florida. My father never packed, we just brought clothes when we got where we were going, but that is another story.

After driving for about 5 minutes daddy turned right on a large dirt driveway. As soon as we turned, I noticed a small house on the left side of the driveway. It was small and just my size. Daddy stopped at the large house at the end of the dirt road. You aren't going to believe who walked outside to meet us, "it was Mrs. Sanders!" I had never seen Mrs. Sanders in any other place other than church. This was exciting! I didn't know that daddy knew Mrs. Sanders. She smiled, said, "hello" and invited us in. I followed as daddy went through the front door. I can't remember much about the inside of Mrs. Sanders's house. However, I do remember it was very nice, warm, and it had lot of different kinds of figurines."

After a few moments she asked if I would like to see the inside of her daughter's doll house. I perked up and replied, "Yes ma'am." She took me to the front door, pointed in the direction of the small house, which was in the front yard. As I got closer to the house, I realized that the house was a prefect size for a 10-year-old. The door, the walls, and the windows were my size. When I opened the door, it was like looking inside of something that couldn't possibility be real, but it was. There were dolls that were dresses to the "nines" and toys galore. Whoever played in the house surely was neat because it seemed that everything had its place. It reminded me right off as being just kind of like Mrs. Sanders's house. I know that she said I could play with anything that I would like, but I really didn't know where to start. There was so much stuff. So, I just watched with true amazement all the girl stuff in the unbelievable prefect sized dollhouse. After just looking a bit, I decided to meander back up to the big house. As I made it to the door Mrs. Sanders and daddy were coming out of the house.

Daddy said, "come on I think you will like what we are going to take a look at." As we made our way around to the backyard I looked to my right and saw a large boat or should I say, "yacht" that looked as though it was just sitting in there "high and dry." As we got closer hear daddy saying, "You have your own railway." Mrs. Sanders remarked, "My husband Mr. Sanders built it so that he could haul his own boat." From where I stood Mr. Sanders did in fact, wherever he was, did pull his 50-foot yacht into their backyard. With the aid of a platform, probably built by the imaginary Mr. Sanders, we boarded the land-loving 50-foot yacht. Now this was the coolest thing I had ever seen.

There was a couch with a coffee table that had nautical lamps attached to each end. Not only that, but they worked. All you had to do was just turn them on. It had a full galley. For those that don't know this is the boat's kitchen. Down below was a stateroom that had a large bed and another room with kind like bunk beds. This was all very cool to a 10-year-old. It seemed from the conversation that Mrs. Sanders wanted to sell the boat or perhaps daddy was interested. I'm not sure, because we never went there again much less brought the boat.

However, there is more to the story. The 50-foot yacht was never moved; it sat there on the railway until it rotted away to a mere pile of metal and wood. I did remember my father suggesting that Mrs. Sanders fill the boat's bilge with water especially if she planned on letting it sit on the railway for a while.

During the wooden boat era, which was where I really got to know boats, things were a lot different. Most boat people or fishermen only had wooden boats. The fact of the matter is "wood it was!" I could go forever about wooden boats and their problems, but I won't. Mrs. Sanders' husband's wooden boat basically rotted totally over the many years that it just sat unattended on the railway.

I would stop while heading out to the ocean to look at Mr. Sanders' decaying yacht. And every time I stopped to look, I would always say, "She was a beautiful classic wooden boat with all the trimmings!" Yep, the wooden boat was truly beautiful. And I bet during its heyday, Mr. Sanders most likely kept it looking prefect!

As far as the Sanders's prefect doll house is concerned, well, it took its toll too! Every time I would ride by in my car, I noticed it had started to spread out more and more. And finally, after many years, the roof caved in. It was a sad day for sure! But you can be sure that I am not the only one that remembers this doll house! I bet the daughters that played there have many grand memories stored up! Why? I only visited the doll house one time, when I was 10 years old, and remember it just like it was only yesterday!

Every year another part of the yacht would cave in to creating a new look. . In the early year of 2000 everything had fallen, the only things left were part of the railway, and some of the metal parts of the old wooden boat. Someone told me when the lot was cleared that they found what was left of a brass lamp buried in some of the yacht's rubble. I can only assume that this was the remains of the brass lamp that I had turned on that really worked when I first boarded Mrs. Sander's imaginary husband's wooden yacht...way back when!

Mrs. Ellie's Crowbar
Wilmington Island's Own Old Local
Watering Hole

Our Crowbar is located on Wilmington Island and has been open for as long as I can remember. My memory started when I was around 5 years old so therefore that would make this establishment about 65 years old. I do remember when the so-called Crowbar was in the fork in the road, not in the shopping center where it is now. Since I was very young at this time here's what I remember about the old Crowbar. They always had live music, well at least when I happened to be there! The band played some interesting instruments. Here's again I am guessing I was about 4 to 5 years old at the time. One of the musicians played a big guitar, which he balanced the fat part down while holding the skinny part up. Most people would have called this a cello. I just called it a deep sound producing kind of playing guitar. Then there was the xylophone, which was the most interesting to me! It was so interesting that daddy brought me one home! As it turned out I really enjoyed trying to make music out of beating the tines! Daddy always said that my music sounded great!

The current owner, Mrs. Ellie Coursey, along with husband Grant Coursey (1941-2003) purchased it in the very early seventies. Anyhow, it has been a meeting/drinking place on Wilmington Island for a very long time. Patrons are waiting in the morning for it to open and are told when it is time to leave when it is closing! So therefore, I would have to say the Crowbar is more than just a local watering hole. It is a place where lots of locals meet along with some outlanders that are known for offering up some interesting facts. After all, facts are the facts!

What is an outlander when associated with the Crowbar? It is an outsider that just walks in that's never seen in the bar! Now this can be a local or a visiting out of Towner. Here are some facts about the Crowbar: There are rules that you must abide by. So, if you act up you might be sentenced to two weeks. What does this mean? You can't come back to the bar for two weeks! Who is your judge and jury? Sometimes the owner, but most of the time the head bartender! There are lots of different timed sentences handed out. My father was sentenced by owner Grant around 1978 with "You can't come back at all!" My father, Captain Sherman I. Helmey's Crowbar sentence when he passed was 15 years old. So therefore, we had my father's wake at the Crowbar, so I guess he did come back after all!

They are known for having the coldest beer in town, which means when they reload those hot ones, they are placed aside so that no patrons are ever served a warm beer. All the food that the Crowbar serves is very delicious! I love this place as well as many others! Now I certainly don't frequent it as much as I used too! However, I kept every darn memory intact!

I remember this just like it was yesterday and before cell phones were even thought of. There was a pay phone hanging on the wall over to the left of the main entrance. I bet "dollars to donuts" that over the many years, while I was there, I used this pay phone at least a dozen times. (912-897-9991) And then there was the time that the feds tapped the pay phone line at Crowbar, because of very interesting conversations that were taking place.

The fact of the matter is many deals from legal to not so legal were discussed over the rotary dialed pay

912-897-9991

phone. As time passed, the pay phone was changed from rotary dialing to push button pay phone! And as more time passed, well, the old pay phone was removed, trying to change once again the old-time great aura that seems to set the pace at the Crowbar!

As you know, even though we were not family, we acted just like them. There were disagreements about all sorts of things, from screaming matches to actual physical showdowns. I remember one time when the receiver was yanked right off the pay phone in Crowbar.

I guess the grabber wanted to use it as a club. It certainly was heavy enough! So, normally when regulars were the ones fighting, sentences would later be handed out. Now if it was an outsider and they were still up right after the encounter, they were barred temporarily and labeled as troublemakers! Here's the bottom line to all of this is thank goodness, not everyone was mad at the same time!

I ran into Mrs. Ellie Coursey the other day and we had a nice conversation. Of course we talked about yesteryear regarding the Crowbar! As we talked, I remember something that happened many years before Mrs. Ellie even owned the bar. And it went something like this:

My father, Captain Sherman I. Helmey, did not like to be told something he didn't want to hear or to do something he did want to do! When daddy did certain things, it had to be his idea!

So, when the preacher came a calling, my father did listen to what he had to say! And when he was finished telling my father that we both needed to be in church on Sunday's and that he wanted my father to agree on a certain amount to give the church. My father always gave money to the church, but on his own cognizance! As I listened even as a young child I kind of knew that this conversation was not going to end well.

So, then my father said, "Since you are treating the church like business, I think I am going to start my own church!" And of course, the preacher replied, "How would that be even possible? Where would you find such a congregation?"

And this is my friend, Chessy Smiling Cat! Some people say, Smiling Cheshire Cat, but daddy did the Chessy Cat Smile! Now you know!

My father was certainly quick on his feet! He simply said, "Well, my plan will be to first start recruiting at the Crowbar!" And the preacher said, "That certainly would not do you any good!" My father replied, "Well, like it or not, but I will get the bulk of your congregation at

my first stop!" Now what could the preacher say? Absolutely not a thing! And what was my father doing? He was sporting an old wild grin, which I had seen many times before! In other words, my father was grinning just like an old Chessy cat!

This was my father before he became Captain Sherman I. Helmey. During the thirties my father was known by most in this era as "Mr. Helmey." According to a story told by one of my father's workers, he had an array of friends wearing expensive shoes, carrying pockets full of money, and driving flashy cars! The fact of the matter is according to this story, daddy's worker moved on early from this situation, because he said, and "I quote," It was much too dangerous of a place to work!

THE FEDS, THE MAIN RASCALS, AND THE OUTSIDE RASCALS

While reading this story you will find that you have the feds, you have the main rascals, and the outside rascals. Over the years I (Captain Judy) as well as my father (Captain Helmey) had plenty of conversations with quite a few FBI agents. In the seventies I remember coming home and finding my father talking to two FBI agents. They were waiting to talk with me, but my father had them at bay about Big Al Capone. I know from that story both agents must have thought they were looking in exactly the right place.

My father, as you know, worked for Big Al Capone during the thirties. I have written dozens of stories about hauling liquor. These stories are based on information that daddy talked about while taking people fishing. Day after day you are bound to remember something. My father told me one thing that I remembered, He said, "I didn't get killed or served any time in jail as a result of my involvement." When it came to hauling any other illegal contraband daddy said, "We are not getting involved!" And we didn't. However, we certainly had the finger pointed at us on more than one occasion. And that is why the FBI agents had stopped by to talk with me.

The questions were always simple, "What were you doing at this time and who with?" I would always have a quick answer, that is if I remembered the time that they were asking about. I knew quite a few so-called fishermen that were allegedly involved in moving contraband from one place to another. Which brings us to this story...

Off the coast in the seventies and eighties quite a bit of drugs hauling and dealing took place in this area. Most of the rascals, since I had best not use names, were very skilled at what they were doing. Back then drug deals were treated somewhat like a business, that's unless something went wrong. And in those days most likely something always goes wrong. Most of the time drug deals were known about by law enforcement way before

90

the deal was done. Take this one time, prior to the invention of the cell phone, where all the transactions were handled directly over the phone. In this case, the phone that the rascals used was a pay phone, which was hanging on the wall at the local watering hole.

And here's how the law found out about this drug deal gone bad before it took place. The drugs were to be brought in by plane. And I really don't know if the plane was going to drop them or land. With supposedly good background information, the rascals approached a certain farmer in the Statesboro area. The owner of the farm agreed for a certain price to allow them to use his field. The deal was seemly so simple! It has always been my thought that the reason most drug deals fail is because too many people are involved. The rascals left Statesboro thinking that this part of the deal was done.

Well, after the farmer thought about it, worried about this, he then contacted the law, and after a little surveillance the feds tapped the pay phone at the local water hole. After this deed was done, it was simply smooth sailing for the feds. All they had to do was listen in on the conversations on the pay phone and wait for the day that the drugs were to be delivered.

Here's where it gets a little sketchy, at least on my part. However, the parts I know about seem to be the most interesting. Since the feds knew everything, I guess it was their decision to decide at what point to stop this drug transaction. I guess from their standpoint to get all that was involved they would have to wait till the deed was almost done. So, the product was delivered to the farm and then it was moved to a large shrimp boat, which strangely enough was renamed Miss Jerry. Since all my father's boats were named Miss Jerry, my father and I both had to scratch our heads on this decision. While everyone was loading the shrimp boat three small boats pulled up alongside. These small boats were also loaded to the hilt. After this deed was done the boats took off. I guess the thought of splitting it up and sending it in different directions made more sense for this move. At dark thirty as soon as the shrimp boat was loaded and still moored at the dock the area was invaded by federal drug agents. All involved couldn't have been more in shock. All were arrested without resistance and the only thing left for the feds was to find out who had weapons or not...And of course two of

91

the small boats that left did not have any idea that the others had been caught. However, so called number three boat did.

Rascals with weapons were charged differently. The bottom line was it was going to be a lot easier for those without guns to plea than those with them. There were couple of rascals that had shotguns in their trucks, and some were packing. However, no guns were ever drawn.

Now for some reason the feds had not intended on smaller boats being involved and since they were taking the shrimp boat before it pushed off watercraft were not included in this bust. So therefore, from their point of view point they had only seen two small boats departing. And the Feds had no water surveillance at this time. The funny thing was no conversations were ever taped about any small boats being involved.

So, here's where it gets so interesting. Let's say for this story's sake that someone in the group had his own personal plan from the start. And let's say, the smaller boats along with their drivers were not known by the rascals on the shrimp boat. And let's say, there was such a large amount of product that they couldn't store it unnoticeably in the shrimp boat. So therefore, they most likely would have left it anyhow. As you can see from reading this story you have the feds, you have the main rascals, and now you have the outside rascals.

The packed full center consoles were so loaded that the drivers of each boat had to push bales aside to arrange peep holes through the high stacks. All boats allegedly headed up the Savannah River under pitch black conditions at speeds of more than 50 knots. Luckily, it was a smooth night, and drivers could focus more on what was ahead instead of having to also beat and pound. Well, it seems the feds did have somewhat of a backup plan, because the coast guard along with other enforcements officers lined the river looking and stopping any boat traffic.

Although I wasn't there let's just say I think I was at least based on the story told. There are things that they say happens when you are on the run from something and that is, "you go into survival mode!" As the three boats made it up the river they separated. And what the two other boats didn't know was that the boat bringing up the rear was forever changing their ongoing plan. As soon as the bringing up the rear boat noticed that the two leads boats had been spotted, he pulled back. He watched as many boats as possible with blinking lights converged on small vessels loaded to the brim with bails of marijuana.

He immediately slowed down and he could feel his heartbeat as though it might just bust right out of his chest. It was at that second; he remembered that he had passed a slow-moving barge about a mile back. He quickly turned around and headed in that direction. As soon as he got to the barge, he knew if he planned this right that this was going to be his only chance of getting past the brigade of boats. And he also knew that if he approached this barge wrong that he wouldn't have to worry about being caught. The outside rascal could have been sucked up under the barge and never be seen again.

Playing out just like a 007 James Bond movie, meaning coming up with the prefect idea and then performing an unbelievable stunt, he sized up the situation as he pulled closer to the starboard side of the barge. Once he picked the perfect spot on the barge, he basically pulled his boat up tight to it. Just like something in the movies, while blending in the barge, he rode right by the coast guard on the water and the feds on the riverbank.

Although he had passed the boats, he knew he was far from being out of the woods. The drop-off location had most likely had been compromised. So, heading in that direction wasn't going to be such a good idea. It was at this time that he knew he was now playing a one-man game. So, he took a detour that would allow him excess to a barrier island that in most cases would not have any sort of visitors. (At least not human ones!) While riding his mind was racing, but he knew he had to focus! Once he arrived at the island he picked a spot, unloaded the pot, and then covered it! He then jumped back in the boat and headed to a place where he could get to land and ditch the boat. The first place that came to mind was the semipublic ramp on Richardson Creek. After reaching this point, he sunk the boat, and started his long walk back to where he was supposed to be in the first place, which was home.

Now why not just ditch the boat and let her float off! Well, by sinking the boat it would help to get rid of any leftovers such as seeds, buds, and leaves out of the boat. Who cares about a few marijuana seeds, buds, and leaves? The feds, especially if they are looking for that missing boat that had been secretly hauling illegal contraband! Did you know that dried seeds, buds, and leaves float when introduced to water? The boat sinks and the contraband are taken away by the wind and tide!

He watched for months as his buddies went on trial one after another with some getting sentences much worse than the others. And there wasn't a day that went by that he didn't look over his shoulder or wonder what that knock on the door was all about. Well, that day never came and the bales that were hidden were never found. Even though he had seemly gotten away with something that most do not, he still had that barrier island and its hidden contents on his mind. He fought with himself about forgetting about it, but he never could get away from that "what if thought." Well, there was one other person involved that could identify him but would never say a thing. So, it was thought maybe he would know what to do...after picking his brain it was decided after a prearranged deal was made it would once again be his turn to move the product. Unfortunately, the product had to be delivered to an old train trestle, which was located up the Savannah River up towards Port Went Worth. Although when it comes to this sort of thing no deal is safe or complete without some sort of problems.

The date was decided and the products got moved up the river to the designated train trestle. Once arriving he was to unload, get paid and then get the heck out of there, which was what he exactly did do. While he was making way back to the dock, he couldn't help but see that someone might be watching. Well, not a thing happened, no one showed up to steal the money or anything like that. When he got home, he separated and packed $100,000.00 dollars into 25 insulated two-quart sealed tea jugs and buried them all in the back yard. He made a pack with himself and his one friend that he would not touch any of this money for a year. His friend who could have called him out during the original bust did not and he took this information with him to the grave!

After one year had passed, he decided to start using some of the money, which he did without prejudice! Moral of the story when it comes to doing the most illegal deals: Always know when it seems almost too simple it is not! When too many are involved more get involved! And if only one other person knew, and he is no longer with us then chances are no one will ever know! And this was the case with outside the small rascal boat number three! Like I always say, "These stories are too darn good to have made up!"

Frankie Fischer is Ms. Joyce's oldest son. Frankie was also raised on Wilmington Island just like me, we never left, and we are still here! Frankie was nice enough to help me with some of the information used in this book. Believe me, he knows some interesting stuff, which was of great help to me!

A big Thanks goes out to Frankie!

Broken off piling going nowhere for no reason!
These were great places to build platforms so the larger boats could
drop them off and the smaller boats would pick them up!

Young's Candy Store

This small building is located next to Mr. and Mrs. Young's home, which is where he raised his family.

Where Wilmington Island Road and North Cromwell meet right across the street sits this small building. It has been many years since this building has been used for anything. Now you might think that this old building was never very important! However, if you did think that, boy you were so very wrong! And let me tell you why! To get this story right I must do some serious digging into my memory banks!

If you are familiar with this area, you have most likely passed by old Young's Marina many times. And maybe or maybe not you might have noticed this building next to the Young's house. But to really tell this story I have to go way back to the beginning, at least the way I remember it..

In the fifties I used to visit Young's Marina all the time. Why? Well, during the season Mr. Young almost always had the prettiest live shrimp in his live wells. When my father wasn't catching his own shrimp, he would send me down to Young's Marina to make a purchase.

Upon this request I would head down to the dock with bucket in hand and jump into my rowboat, which was powered by a 31/2 horsepower Evinrude outboard. And make way to Young's Marina, which was located about 6 docks down from our place.

Once I motored into an empty dock space, I tied her up, grabbed my bucket, and headed up to the top of the dock to purchase daddy some live shrimp. I remember always being a little intimidated as I made my way up the ramp! It seemed Mr. Young was always at the dock when I arrived. As soon as I made it to the top of the ramp he would always smile and ask if he could help me. After explaining that I was Captain Helmey's daughter and that I was sent to purchase some live shrimp. It was at this time he pointed to the tanks and told me to help myself.

My father always told me to only get a quart. That way there would most likely always be some left for the next fishermen. After dipping my shrimp, I would walk over and always try to hand Mr. Young $2.00, which he would never ever take. Now that I think about it Mr. Young never took any sort of payment from me!

There were always lots of people hanging around at Young's marina. He let people fish off his floating docks, which offered up many different fishing spots. He also rented wooden row boats, oars, boat cushions, and small outboard engines. All his wooden boats were very clean and always freshly painted. He painted all his boat battleship gray, and each had a number on it. I always wondered why he numbered them, but after thinking about it, I got it!

Years later, after the passing of Mr. Young, I stopped by to visit Mrs. Young. As we talked about this and that she told me that when her husband passed that my father did not go to the funeral. Mrs. Young said, "I was really upset with him!

The fact of the matter is Captain Helmey never came by until about a week afterwards! And when he arrived, Mr. Young really gave him the cold shoulder. Your father gave his condolences and offered a reason why it took so long. Your father said that he waited until all the company and family left because he felt I would really need more then! With that being said I forgave him and thanked him for his thoughtfulness!

As a small child, in the fifties, my father used to take me down to Mr. Young's Candy Store, which was located right next to his home. Now you are talking about real candies and delicious cookies Mr. Young had them for sure! The ones I remember the most are small cake type squares made of shredded coconut that were covered with different color icings. There was always an assortment of cookies, which as you guessed were made with real butter for sure! I can still remember the taste and when I do real darn butter comes to mind! All the candies and cookies were displayed in big clear round glass containers with heavy tops.

I couldn't pick the lids up! So, I had to wait for daddy to stop talking long enough to do it for me. And as soon as he did, I could pick out exactly what I wanted. It was always too good to be true! And then one day, the store never opened again, and the building just sat there. I often wondered if the big jars were still in there! And if I went that far. I guess I most likely thought about what might be in them too!

When both Mr. and Mrs. Young passed their daughter moved down to the old Marina home. And just as I had done years before I stopped in for a visit with Mr. and Mrs. Young's daughter! She was very nice, and you know we had to talk about the old days! It is what we do when we get older, we talk about the past. Mr. Young's daughter told me that her father basically made the marina a fine learning tool for the children. It was their job to help get the boat cushions, bait, crab lines, oars, etc. to the customers. And that was not all they had to add up the costs so that they could properly and correctly charge the customers. She told me that each item that they rented was priced separately. She said sometimes this was a terrible task while other times it was lots of fun!

The whole time I was listening to her I was thinking about the little candy shop outside and all the memories of the lost tastes that went with it. And you know I had to ask, "Why did you father close the best candy store in the world?" She quickly answered, "Someone spat on the floor and my father closed the doors forever!" And the bottom line is I certainly did not see that coming! Did you?

Exactly How Many Boats Were Sunk?

Somewhere between the late sixties and early seventies while eating at Tassey's Pier located in Thunderbolt, Georgia my father got to see and hear some interesting things. While eating his appetizer crab cake, which at the time Tassey Salas was the

TASSEY'S PIER

Did it happen or not at Tassey's Pier in the late sixties or early seventies!

first restaurant that came up with this. Normally when you order crab it comes in the form of what is better known as a deviled crab, which was made very famous by Williams Seafood!

While my father was occasionally gazing out the window at the water, having a few drinks, and telling a few stories, a crowd of around 10 people walked into the restaurant. This crowd was loud and very angry about the fact that the Hotel (Savannah Inn aka Oglethorpe Hotel) had denied their reservations, which they had confirmed months ago. They had their paperwork and everything they needed once arriving at the hotel, proving that they had reservations. However, their 5 room's double occupancy reservations were denied, and they were turned away.

The Savannah Inn is also known as the Sheraton Hotel but better known back in the old days as the Oglethorpe Hotel! The hotel was located on Wilmington Island and had the Wilmington River as their backyard. Originally the hotel had a large double floating dock, which was quite frequently used by its patrons. And of course, there were those sometimes drop-offs and pick-ups, which I don't know too much about, or I just don't want to write about yet, but sooner or later it is going to come out!

Why did I happen to think about this, I had some people on the boat this past week that were working at the front desk of the Savannah Inn (old Oglethorpe Hotel) when the Augusta boat Club came to stay at the hotel. According to this conversation, the group had truly prepaid and everything! However, the people at the front desk were instructed by their boss to deny them excess. When the group arrived the hotel front desk person even after looking at confirmed paperwork said, "I am sorry, but your rooms are not available!" Of course, the group had all their pre-payment paperwork hand. However, even with proof of a 5-room reservation the hotel staff immediately asked the group to leave, which they angrily did!

This ten-person group had traveled by boat from Augusta down the Savannah River in a caravan. They were supposed to spend the weekend at the hotel. As you can imagine, when they left, they were very mad, and most likely drinking might have been involved! It was quickly decided to roll a golf cart and quite a few pieces of furniture into the large, beautiful swimming pool!

As they made way down the dock to their boat it was decided that they would all head over to Tassey's pier to eat. After all, Tassey's had plenty of dock space where all 5 boats could comfortably tie up. This was a great place to go by boat or car to eat, which was in Thunderbolt. The restaurant was owned by Tassey Salas, and he became a noted restaurateur until his retirement in 1983! Mr. Tassey was known for his warm hospitality when greeting his patrons with a joke! He was always very nice to my father and me.

After trying to decide on their next move, eating lots, and of course drinking more, they went down to their boats. What did they find? All five boats were sunk but still tied to the dock! A strong message was sent, "Don't mess with us or we will mess with you!"

You have read about what I do know about this story for instance. So, if anyone knows anything else, please contact Captain Judy 912 429 7671 or email fishjudy2@aol.com.. The source will not be published unless you like me too!

This is a picture of a 1970's Tommy gun type with a silencer!

I do not know how the boats were sunk or if the police were called. I can't describe the scene that took place when the group walked down to their boats. I really wanted to say that the sinking took place do to the Tommy gun spray of bullets lined above each boat's water line. But if that much shooting had taken place someone would have heard it or not! Or maybe they used silencers. And with that thought, I looked on the web and found some pictures of Tommy guns with silencers that could have possibly been used during the 1970's Gangster era! I am not a private eye, but I think I just solved the big question of how the sinking was done! Your thoughts?

Big Mystery Still!

It is a big mystery regarding Jimmy Hoffa's disappearance! Mr. Hoffa was an important man before his disappearance, but even more after!

Jimmy Hoffa Is Missing

To bring you up to speed regarding this story I need to make you aware of some certain interesting things. My father officially worked for Big Al Capone during the years 1930 through 1933. Even after most of my father's so-called illegal operations stopped after prohibition, I still think that he was still connected somewhat to the grand mafia underworld! So, after finding out what I am about to share with you I wasn't the only one that thought he might still be a little connected even in 1975!

The grandson of US Marshall Ancil Gordon chartered a boat and went fishing with Captain Garrett Ross of Miss Judy Charters on Monday September 29, 2024. Kerry Parker was the grandson of Ancil Gordon, our neighbor, and a serious appointed member with the US Marshall Service. Now, don't worry, I am trying to pull this information together and it should make some sense soon. US Marshall Gordon was our neighbor for as long as I can remember. Gordon's house and dock were located only a few doors down from our house. Quite often when Kerry would visit his grandfather's he would swim to our dock to see us (My father Captain Sherman aka Moose Helmey and me (Captain Judy Helmey) This is just about where Kerry became Jerry. For many years, I thought Kerry's name was Jerry! Now that you get the just of all of this you should understand better why I am telling you this interesting new story.

When Kerry arrived to go fishing, we had a great conversation. He told me that his US Marshall grandfather had a picture of himself and Jimmy Hoffa, which was taken at their dinner table. Kerry told me that his grandfather had been assigned to help Mr. Hoffa or should I say, "Be a buddy guard!" Yes, a buddy, not a bodyguard! So therefore, Mr. Hoffa joined US Marshall

Gordon and his wife for dinner at their house. I asked Kerry, also known as Jerry by me mostly, could I please have a copy of this picture. Well, unfortunately, this picture went missing many years ago and hasn't been seen since. Darn, Darn and Darn!

As we were walking down to the boat Kerry looked at me and said, "My grandfather told me that after Jimmy Hoffa was deemed officially among the missing that he made an appointment with my father!" And of course I had to ask, why? And this is what Kerry Said, "My grandfather US Marshall Gordon wanted to ask your father Captain Sherman "Moose" Helmey if he could share any information on the whereabouts of Jimmy Hoffa!"

Since I wasn't present when this question was asked, I don't know exactly what my father said! However, it couldn't have been much, because as we all know Jimmy Hoffa is one of the most missing people that we really didn't know much about until he disappeared!

The Tailor Louis Frank Rosanova "The Tailor" 1922-2003 made this interesting call! After doing a little checking and reading this great book, "Mob Island by Bubba Haupt and Ph.D. Teresa E. Ward!" I was made aware that Mr. Rosanova might have said, "Sewing just calms his darn nerves!" You need to purchase a copy of Mob Island!

Room 206 Savannah Inn and Country Club

Everything Went Up in Smoke!

This allegedly happened during the 1970's at the Savannah Inn and County Club Era! It was pretty much local common knowledge that the Savannah Inn, also known by us old codgers as the Oglethorpe Hotel, was so-called not so secretly run by the mafia from the mid 30's to the 70's! And if you have been reading my stories you already know that it is official that my father worked for big Al Capone in the 30's! So, a lot of this written information that I am sharing came straight from stories continuously told by my father, which later as we all found out were basically true! Now that was a mouth full!

So, this friend of mind in the mid-seventies worked at Savannah Inn as the pool boy. As time moved on, Frank (not his real name) not only worked at the pool, but also gained another job. He became the big man's bartender. In this story, the big man, was the one that took care of any mafia business that was brought to the hotel. Now, the big man didn't necessarily run it, he hired people to take care of that job. However, it was his hotel to do when, what, and why whenever he wanted! I think it would have been a hard job to be hired as this hotel's manager! Why? Because the right way was their way, which meant as this hotel manager you most likely could never be right!

On this day, the pool phone rang, Frank answered it, and said hello! On the other end was the Big Man! And He said, "Frank, cleanup room 206 and get back to me when it's done!" The guest cut his hand and is now being transported to the hospital." Thinking not a thing of this request, Frank said, "I will take care of it!"

Frank had just returned from lunch and after taking care of a few things for the pool he headed to the main lobby. He stopped by the main lobby desk, picked up the key for room 206, and headed upstairs. He grabbed the doorknob, inserted the key, turned it, and the door opened. As Frank walked into the room his brain couldn't believe the images his eyes were sending!

He stopped onto his tracks and took it all in. At first all he could think was, boy this guest must have really cut himself. As he scanned the room, his thoughts changed, but he didn't want to admit it even to himself. There was blood everywhere from the walls to the bed, to the dresser to the bathroom. It was quite a sight for sure.

He had been instructed to burn everything that had any remnants of blood. It was a good thing that the hotel has its own incinerator, because this job was going to require a lot of incinerating! After Frank's soaring blood pressure dropped back to normal, he started better assessing the situation. There was one thing for sure, he was not going to be able to accomplish this by himself. In other words, he would need help! With that thought in mind, Frank would have to decide who that someone could be. This meant two someone's that would do what was needed with prejudice. Prejudice in this case means just do the work, don't talk about it, keep your opinions to yourself, and don't think about it. Any talking, thinking, or questioning regarding this incident by people doing the cleaning certainly would not end well!

After thinking about who the best helpers would be, he made the call and asked them to come up to room 206. He met the two helpers outside the room so that he could explain in a short version the kind of what they were walking into! Since both helpers knew about the code of silence and being barred from asking questions, Frank's explanation was a short one. The story went something like this, Frank said, "A guest severely cut their hand opening a window and had to be transported to the hospital."

After the shock of walking into the room wore off the work began. Everything pretty much had to go from the linens to the drapes to carpets to the towel to the dollies on the tables! In other words, everything that could and did absorb anything of a liquid nature! (Trying to keep the word BLOOD out of it! Apparently, there was a lot of this to go around and it did!) All furniture had to be washed and then wiped down. When all these tasks were properly performed Frank sent the two helpers back to their now boring other hotel jobs.

He then called the big man to report in and to ask a simple question. And that was, I just opened the closet and the guest's clothes were still hanging. Frank asked, "Do you want me to pack them up?" Big man quickly replied, "Burn them!" (As soon as this came out of his mouth the phone went dead!)

With that being the next job, he quickly grabbed all the clothes and started throwing them in the push buggy. All of them had pushed this buggy to the incinerator many times on this day. The best news is that one more time to the incinerator and Frank's job would be done. Once the closet was emptied, he began to open drawers to make sure all the clothes were removed. In the last dresser drawer were two very nice colorful silk shirts, which were still in the packaging that they were purchased in. Upon seeing these beautiful shirts, Frank quickly decided, what the heck? I am going to keep these, and he did!

After arriving home that evening, Frank quickly opened the packaging, took one of the shirts out, and put it on. To his amazement, the silk shirt was so big that it almost swallowed him. All Frank could think now was this was a big man that cut his hand for sure! And then Frank said, the most correct way to end this story is to say, the silk shirts were so large that they would have fit big Luca Brasi who played Bodyguard/hitman in movie Godfather! While we were on this subject, I did a little checking. Did you know that Luca Brasi (Lenny Montana real name was a x-pro wrestler) before he was discovered was hired on the movie set to be security guard.

And regarding this story, I was told by a confident source that there most likely were more than one person put to rest or better said, "Taken apart!" in room 206! And that is all I am going to say about this story!

When a hotel was discussed, this was the one they came up with! Yep, we would be locked up in a room with a guard at the door! Now I must ask you, how stupid do you think we are?

HOTEL HOLD UP

During this time drug deals at the local water hole things were getting a little on the wild side. The local bar was called the "Old Crowbar now called Elie's Crowbar!" It has had this name for as long as I have been around in the reading mode, which is about fifty plus years. I was asked many times to join in on the so-called fun party. After all I had a boat, knew how to run it, especially at night, and could have been an asset to the group.

However, I just couldn't keep the possibility of "jail time" out of my mind. At any rate, my father as well as myself were contacted on many occasions and explained this so called "fool proof plan." I as well as my father listened to the desires of the person on the other end of the phone. Here's what their proposal consisted of:

The first thing and funniest of the conversation was the fact that they tried to disguise their voices, which in this case was the same as wearing a hooded cape while wearing the same old dirty shoes. (Once again, another story that has yet to be told!) We would say hello and absolutely no real or fake name would be offered up. At this point laughing was out of the question. As with every call, the whole fiasco considered would be already planned out. We would be paid "X" amount of money. For this money, we weren't to report that our boats had been stolen one week after they were missing from the dock. To make sure that nothing went wrong from our end we were to meet at an unknown location, which is not revealed now. Once arrived at the "destination stop" we (daddy and I) we would be heavily monitored until notification of final analysis. I just had to put all of this "mojo" language in this story, because they believed that what they were doing was legal business. I suspected that some of their big heads were just about to explode with power.

At any rate, the short version of what we had to do was so simple but explained as complicated as possible. Before our boats were purposefully stolen, we were to be locked up in a guarded hotel room until the drug hauling to unknown parts had taken place. If all went well our boats would be returned unharmed or scuttled, at which time we could report this to our insurance company. My father and I might have been just plain old fishermen. However, we did know what smelled fishy and, on a hook, when we were presented with one!

My father being a wise old man decided quickly that this wasn't a job that we were interested in. While talking with the so-called "not known person" on the other end, my father acted as if he didn't and would have never understood a thing that the person said or had asked. After I thought about it, it might have been fun, of course, if we hadn't been caught by the feds or shot by the drug smugglers. The bottom line of this story is the fact that what sounds good sometimes isn't!

Captain Helmey Times Two!

Here we have Captain Judy Lynn Helmey and her father Captain Sherman Israel Helmey, sometimes referred to back in the old days as Moose Helmey!

This picture was taken as my father was opening his many birthdays presents. This was one of his early seventy's birthday parties, which most likely ended with several blue light specials in the yard. You see, there was a serious amount of food, lots of liquor, and beer consumed! And believe you me two of these three things when over indulged can change the course of an evening quick!

A Homemade Colorful Crocheted Peter Warmer!

On this birthday my father received one of the most unusual gifts. One of his girlfriends, maybe current at the time or not, crocheted him a peter warmer! As you can see from the picture above it looks like what it is. A crocheted peter warmer! As my father opened this present and then took a good look, the expression on his face was priceless! I told daddy, it is just a joke gift! With a straight face his reply was, "I certainly don't need one of those!" Believe me, he was serious for all the right reasons!

The Family Tree

My last name is Helmey. There are also Helmly's, which are also related to our clan. However, it has been a mystery for years the reason behind why one family spells their name Helmey while others in the family spell its Helmly. Many years ago, my father told me it was over religion, which brings me to my next story!

Are You Related or Not?

The good Old Helmey Name or not!

While talking with Jeff Whitten of the Bryan County News many years ago he remembered a story that was told to him, which was original for sure! As we talked, he asked, "Where's is your family from?" I answered, "Effingham County." Then I mentioned that Colic Helmey Road was named after my grandfather. This reply brought to the conversation table a very interesting story, which I had never heard before. Since it was basically about my family to say the least, I was very interested. Jeff then asked, "Was I related to the Helmey's or Helmly's?" I answered quickly with "yes," and then I proceeded to give him what I thought was the reasoning behind the change from either "E's to L's or vice versa!" I never took a breath with the answer and said, "I was always told it was basically about religion!" However, I always thought in the back of my mind, knowing some of my family as I do, such as my father mainly, that it might be over a woman. With that all being said, Jeff shared with me what he was told by someone many years ago! He couldn't remember his source's name, which was fine with me. I would rather ask for forgiveness later! Although the source left Jeff's mind his memory of the story did not. After you read you will understand why! The story went like this:

According to the source, it was never ascertained which name "Helmey or Helmly" came first. Not even I know that one. And the person that could have probably told me, who is my Aunt Hattie, is no longer with us. Apparently, a Helmey or Helmly family member stole a pig from another family member, which really upset the entire so call "family clan." To distinguish the "pig stealing" side of the family, the pig stealers were forced to change the "E to L or maybe the L to E.!" This change was made so that future generations would know, which side of the family was the "pig swiping side!" The rest is history!

I asked Jeff would it be OK to reveal my source and reluctantly said "yes, but with concerns!" He just didn't want any of the family members to be upset with him. I assured him that no one would be mad!

Now that this subject has been brought to light and since I am from the "Helmey side" I really don't know what to think regarding "pig swiping!" I certainly can't say for sure that it wasn't my side of the family because I really don't know! However, I will proclaim that since my father worked for Big Al, often was involved in so-called shady deals even though he was never actually caught, was married eight plus times, but never stopped dating, drank a fifth of liquor almost every day between the hours of five and seven, and I could go on, but I must stop somewhere. My point being is that I don't think, at least based on my father's track record, that my family had the time much less cared to "swipe a pig!" Thanks, Jeff, for remembering and sharing one heck of a story! You are the best!

HELMEY CEMETERY!

The Helmey family has their own cemetery in Effingham. My Aunt Hattie had bodies excavated way back when, because she found out that they were not a true Helmey. Or better yet, she did not consider them Helmey for long enough! I wished had more information about this, but after the last body excavation, no one dared ask!

DADDY'S PARENTS!

My grandparents on daddy's side (Captain Sherman Israel Helmey).
Kolic Israel Helmey (1868-1949) Married Lelia Mell Hester (1807-1959)

Now we have Helmey's, and Hester's and Mell's incorporated!
A little later as marriages took place the Zipperer's, Ambrose's,
Hinely's and Bagley's

I never met Granddaddy Kolic. As a child and up till I was
around 8 years old I visited my grandmother at her home. I
played on the porch that's shown in the background of this
picture. I can still remember all the other structures around the
house. My grandmother had a smoke house, tool house, barn,
and several other cottages where families lived that worked on
the farm. It was certainly a grand place for a child to play.

KOLIC HELMEY ROAD

This is where it all started in 1868! If you want to visit you can find Kolic Helmey Road and Earl Lain Road in Effingham, Georgia.

My aunt Hattie was commissioned to have this road named after her father Kolic Helmey, who was my grandfather. My aunt had the road sign changed three times, because the county never could get Kolic spelled correctly. Heck, it seems no one knew the correct spelling except my aunt and the old family

bible! According to the story, my aunt took the family bible, made a copy of the family page, and sent it to those that had the power to change the sign. This is the number three sign! I guess you could say, "Three times the charm!"

As of this day and time we have got a street named after my grandfather and a place named after Aunt Hattie! And there are several schools also!

Big Farm in Effingham!

My father's family owned a big farm in Effingham, Georgia, which was located west of Savannah. The area where he was raised was always referred to as "Scuffle Town."

According to the family tree, my father had three brothers and three sisters. I only knew two of daddy's sisters, Aunt Ida and Aunt Hattie. As far as his brothers, I knew Uncle Randal and Uncle Mac. When I was very young, I remember meeting my father's mother. It's funny what you remember about older people that you met when you were young. I remember my grandmother had long dark and light gray hair that she would tie up in a bun. And I also remember that she could cook some of the best country style dishes that I ever tasted! And I didn't even have to add ketchup!

Since they were raised on a farm, they all had chores. However, my Uncle Randall said, "Your father would do anything to get out of doing his share!" When Daddy and I went to Uncle Randall's house for dinner this was always the big joke at the table. Now that I think about it, my father was the biggest of all his brothers and sisters with my Uncle Randall being the smallest of them all. Uncle Randall always said, "It's because I did all the work while your father watched or just goofed off!"

Later in life I was told the reason why Uncle Randal was so small. It was because as a child he had been bit by a rattle snake and almost died. It was at this time I figured it wasn't daddy at all, it was that darn snake that must have stunned his growth.

My Uncle Ed was really my cousin. He was my father's sister's child. And my father and Uncle Ed had great fun hunting, fishing, and finding themselves in some good clean trouble. They both smoked big cigars, shared the same great opinions, and practiced old school ways quite frequently. My Uncle Ed was truly more than a local legend!

*In 2018 the new King George Boulevard Bridge
was named after Senator Edward H. Zipperer*

*Cheers to all! Uncle Ed with his big cigar! It's a family tradition! According
to his daughter Laura, her father's inscription on his tie sends a direct message.
The script spells out "BULL SHIP!" (Or something close to that! In other
words, replace the P with a T!)*

Uncle Ed was always practicing old school tactics!

Now I am sure you are thinking, what the heck does that mean? Well, I will try to explain. Many years ago, I was having some business issues with the county. Well, it's not like I was doing anything different regarding the fishing business that we started in 1948. However, trying to get this point across to a panel of official people that didn't know anything about us was at best a pain in my asteroid!

With that thought in mind, I decided to go see my uncle who really was my cousin. Uncle Ed was a retired US State Senator and negotiator with many contacts in the know, that could most likely convince and conclude! And it went something like this: I told uncle my problem and he said, "I will meet you at the courthouse in the morning!"

So, as I was waiting inside the courthouse the next morning, Uncle Ed walked up smoking a big cigar. And he said, "I will be back in the minute!" I watched as he smoked his big cigar right in the courthouse and walked through a door that had "No admittance" in big red letters across it.

About 20 minutes later, Uncle Ed walked out the same door he entered. This time he was smoke free and while looking at his watch, he said, "I have to go, I have a tee-time in an hour in Hilton Head!" And then he nodded, winked, and headed to his waiting car!

Senator Ed Zipperer (1931-2024) his daughter Laura, and Ed's father Forrester Zipperer!

I was still standing in the same spot while waiting for my meeting where I was worried that my head was going to be placed on the proverbial chopping block. And so, the meeting began with a councilman stating the list of reasons for this gathering. My name, of course, came up a lot. Then the meeting took a mundane course, and a few more incidental things were addressed about my company. And then someone said, "Miss Judy Charters has been doing business for many years without any problems. And we suggest that this should continue, and she has our complete approval!"

My Uncle might not have gotten a hole in one at the golf course on this day, but he certainly did in the meeting! So therefore, in my case, here's where a little smoke, big smile, and wink got the job done! Now if you don't understand the old school ways then you must be too darn young to do so!

This happened over 30 years ago! And as of this year (2025) our company, which started out as Captain Helmey's charter boat company and then became Miss Judy Charters, has been serving customers for 77 years! And this is my (Captain Judy's) 60th year personally taking customers fishing!

Georgia State Senate! (Uncle Ed served on senate 1967-1975)
Senator Uncle Ed Zipperer handing over important papers to Ms. Edna Pierce
(secretary to Senator Hugh Gillis)

119

RATTLE SNAKES CAN'T JUMP, BUT THIS ONE DID!

As with all good family stories, this one also has what could be called a hook-up kind of ending. According to this family story my father was the one that told Uncle Randall (as a small child) that he could make the jump across the ditch. My father also said, "Don't worry about that snake, just jump over it!" And of course, Daddy also said, "Snakes cannot jump!" Now you know the rest of the story!

Captain Sherman I. Helmey and his sister Hattie Helmey Zipperer. They are sitting on a bench at the Cracker Barrel located on Highway 204 and I-95. When Highway 204 was constructed, it ran right through my Aunt Hattie's property. Aunt Hattie used to say all the time while sitting on this bench that her property line was only a few yards away! You see the front door of the Cracker Barrel was located about 75 feet from her property. At the time she was very right. She owned property on both sides of the road that ended at the Cracker Barrel!

The Great Beef Cow Movement!

According to Aunt Hattie, her cows did not appreciate all the changes either! The location of the road cut her cow pastures right in half! So now she had beef cows on both sides!

My father's older sister Hattie, who was married to Forrest Zipperer, was more of a grandmother to me than an aunt. Aunt Hattie was a fine southern lady and was considered the matriarch of the family in more ways than one. Now we can add Zipperer's to the family mix of Helmey's, Hester's and Mell's incorporated) And before this is all over said and done, I will add Ambrose to the list of family names. My aunt Ida married John David Ambrose, better known by me as Good old, but very tall Uncle Sam! This could have been my rendition due to the fact I was so young as well as short and Uncle Sam was just big as well as very tall!

My family was an interesting bunch for sure. I am familiar and feel most comfortable talking about Helmey's and Zipperer's side. Let's start with the Zipperer side of the family. They were big farmers, had big dairies, and cattle people. Not only that, but they also own and leased lots of land and had become pretty darn powerful people. Basically, they were good darn powerful people! Edward H. Zipperer's, (1931-2024) Hattie and Uncle Forrester's son became a US Senator and served from 1967-75. Judging from the many great things he accomplished for the people I would say, "We got our money's worth with this senator!"

Well, the very interesting Helmey's side of my family is exactly what this book is all about! Helmey's size spun some big ones for sure. From gangsters to hijackers, heroes, to some serious fishers!

PEACOCKS!

Throughout the book there are several stories about my Aunt Hattie. As I can recall when Aunt Hattie spoke, people mostly listened. Now there were a few like my father that would listen, but that was about the end of it. She always told my father that he partied too much and dated all the wrong kind of women. Aunt Hattie has a name for those women, and she called them "Peacocks!" (These were women not birds. Just in case you were wondering!) As a child I thought it was funny, but never really understood why.

Kim Burge, Uncle Mac's granddaughter, found these matchbook cover!

My father's younger brother was Sylvester McRae Helmey. I called him Uncle Mac, he owned the first lumber mill in Savannah, Georgia. It was called the Savannah Planing Mill. He married Freida Waters, and they had a son that they named Robert, who was better known to all of us as "Big Reds." Uncle Mac was a very successful lumber business and was a member in high standing of the international Concatenated Order of the HOO-HOO. I gave them another name. From now on the HOO-HOO was better known as the Lumber Mafia!

My cousin "Reds" who I called Uncle Bobby was a decorated member of the armed forces running covert missions, which thank goodness we can now finally talk about.

1919 Model T Ford

The family's first car..

When my father's parents purchased their first car, it was at that time that my father knew he wasn't going to be a farmer but instead an automobile mechanic. According to history the automobile put into motion plenty of changes. My father loved a good challenge and trying to fix everything wrong with a car was going to be one heck of a quest!

The family car made one heck of a hit with my father. He told me that he took the car apart at least dozens of times just to see how it worked. My Aunt Hattie told me that my father's only desires were to work on that darn car. (And Aunt Hattie rarely used the word darn.) When it came to my father doing chores it was out of the question.

With the family having only one car it was hard to get a chance to use it, that's, unless you came up with a plan. Daddy always told his father that the car was broken and that he was working on it. Aunt Hattie would always say, "Sherman you know how

123

that car got broke; you did it taking it apart!" My father seemed to always get his way when it came to the family car. He just couldn't keep his hands off it. According to Aunt Hattie his head was under the hood while his feet were always sticking straight up.

With daddy's always saying the car was broken, it gave him plenty of freedom to work on it all day. My Aunt Hattie said, "Your father also had another trick when it came to getting complete control of the family car!" Daddy would tell his father as well as all his siblings not to drive the car, because it was broken. Then there was this one day where according to Aunt Hattie it wasn't broken, and she was going to prove it. On this day when daddy said, "The car is broken and don't drive it!" Aunt Hattie talked Uncle Randall into giving the car a try anyway. Uncle Randall said, "Sherman said the car was broke!' Aunt Hattie replied, "Let's find out I bet it is not!" After being pushed into it, Uncle Randall got in the car and got ready to crank it. My father was hiding behind the barn all the while watching as this cranking of the car unfolded. Sure enough, Uncle Randall cranked the car and when he did a loud explosion came up under the hood, fire shot out the sides of the car, and one side of the hood completely blew off.

Uncle Randall flew out of the car as if he had wings attached. Aunt Hattie just held her mouth with hopes that Randall had not got hurt. And my father who heard the explosion walked up and said, "I told you the car was broke!" This one sentence puts my father back in the driver's seat along with scaring everyone in the family from wanting to ever drive the car.

Just to set the record straight my father finally told his sister and brother what he had done to the car, but it took some 20 years plus to come clean. My father told them that he had taken a gas-soaked rag and stuffed it in the carburetor. Then he took the screws out of the right side of the hood with hopes that it wouldn't fall off until it was time! My father was a rascal!

BIG CITY OF SAVANNAH!

By the time daddy turned eighteen he had skipped his way through high school and even attended a little college. However, absolutely none of this so-called schooling seemed to get his attention. According to him, he hadn't learned a thing! So, in the early twenties my father left home. He had decided that neither getting schooled nor farming was how he wanted to make a living. As my father left home his mother handed him $25.00 dollars, which was to help him find his future in the big city!

The big city that I am talking about is Savannah, Georgia. My father told me that during the twenties $25.00 was a lot of money, but he knew he had to find work as quickly as possible. Since he knew all about the family car and loved working on it, so much, he started with the automobile repair shops. Of course, the first question was always, where have you worked before and where did you get your experience? Those asking did so with a strong smile while almost laughing in daddy's face. The repair shop owners already knew that my father was much too young to have any experience in repairing an automobile. Well, they were certainly wrong for sure!

After so many rejections he decided on a new approach. After introducing himself to the next repair shop, he offered his automobile repairs services for one week with no set pay. It was decided by handshake that at the end of the week, an agreement would be made on whether he had the job. According to daddy the automobile repair industry was so new that those that seemed that they knew how to fix a car did not.

With his new plan daddy was able to secure a job without pay for one week. My father knew as soon as they saw him working on a car that they would quickly change their minds and hire him for sure. During his first week, he did the work of three mechanics. Daddy already knew more about cars than most mechanics. This was since he had done so much work on the family car. (And that was whether it was needed or not!) With this prior self-taught learning my father knew cars backwards and forwards, bringing to light that a new job could be in his future. My father could disassemble and reassemble a complete car in two days. At the end of the week my dear old dad was hired not fired!

Now that daddy had a job he set his sights on a new goal, which was to work hard and save money so that he could start his own business! I really can't remember how long it took daddy to get to the "in his own business situation." However, it did happen, and his business was called "Helmey's Garage!"

THE REST OF THE STORY IS HEARSAY OR MAYBE IT'S THE DARN TRUTH!

My father's first daughter Merceles Helmey Bagley.

Somewhere between the first job and the start of his new business my father got married. This first marriage was the beginning of many. My father and his first wife Louise were gifted with a baby girl, who they named Merceles.

It's strange what you remember when you start thinking about the old times. As a small child I remember Louise as being one of my aunts not my father's ex-wife. To make all this even more creepy, I spent lots of time with Aunt Louise. Daddy would drop me off and I would spend the day with Aunt Louise! I always had a wonderful time. I would pick out the sheet music, which was stacked in her piano bench! Once I made my selection, she would play the piano and we both would sing sing sing and sing some more! It was a good time for sure!

127

His daughter Merceles married Calvin Bagley! They had two children!

Please meet Cindy and Cheryl! My father's grandchildren. My nieces are so precious!

When my father and Louise got divorced lots of things changed, but not so much! According to those in the know, my father was never home that much when he was married to Louise, which lasted about 21 years. According to most, he never stopped dating! In the divorce decree my father gave Louise the home that they were living in, which was 1104 East 40th Street in Savannah. It also states that she got a 1943 Desoto car, and whatever ownership they had in Oscheig Breckridge florist. And of course, there was permanent alimony involved, for sure. Now, when I was around 6 years old, right after my mother's death, I spent lots of time with Aunt Louise. (He was married to Louise the first wife for a mere 21 years, then he married my mother, and after her death, he was married about 4 to 6 more times.) Let me put this into perspective for you as the reader: Before I was the age of 16, I had at least 4 to 6 stepmothers. The longest my father was ever married to Louise, which was 21 years. The shortest time in marital wed lock was 6 weeks.

To be honest, I really don't know how my father had time to get all the big business things accomplished that he did. As well as all the marriages and divorces that took place before, during, and after it is said as well as done. Lots of moving parts when it comes to like, love, marriage, and then divorce.

I remember four attorneys in my father's life: In the earlier days there was John Calhoun and Robert Duffy! Then in the newer days Joe Bergen and his son Fred Bergan took care of all of daddy's needs and mine too! I don't remember entering the front door of these offices, we always entered the back door to most of these offices. Just putting into words everything that my father accomplished from age 21 until his death in 1993 is going to take another book just to explain. The name of the book could have a very long title. And it might go something like this...Daddy the mechanic, the businessman, the Gangster, the charter boat captain, and the complete womanizer in every way that's possible!

Divorce A Vinculo
Matrimonial Number One

Speaking of my father's many failed marriages, I need to share with you the interesting parts of each one.

His first marriage to Louise lasted 21 years and I truly believe my father never stopped dating! After reading all the details in regard to information the courts required them to come to a decision on the best divorce decree for both was seriously mind-boggling!

Over their 21 years of marriage my father and his first wife (Louise) acquired/owned/rented 8 residences, ran/owned Helmey's garage, and ran/owned Helmey's filling station, which had 10 employees.

This photo was taken in the late thirties or early forties. My father (Mr. Sherman I. Helmey wearing a white shirt) is leaning next to the wrecker. Helmey's Garage was located on the corner of Oglethorpe and Montgomery streets. (Present day, where the Chatham County jail and courthouse sits!) To the right of this picture was Hudson-Helmey Used Cars! According to my Uncle Bobby aka "Reds," daddy's nephew before it was Helmey's Garage it was a Jewish Synagogue. And then there is the building behind it which was considered a Whore House before and most likely after. (Especially, if my father had anything to do with it!) I do remember daddy telling me a story about giving free electricity to the ladies of the evening and telling the Savannah Electric to take their poles off his property! This is one of my father's properties that was listed in his first 1943 divorce paperwork.

HE SAID, SHE SAID

She (Lousie) said, "Separation was due to mental cruelty such as fussing, abusing, cursing, and threatening!" According to records, my father had a distasteful disposition and from the time of marriage, fussed and nagged continually, making life miserable. Once he became angry, he called her unspeakable names, making it very embarrassing and humiliating for her. On more than several occasions he threatened her, causing serious apprehension for the safety of her life, limb, and health! And she feels that a restraining order is necessary due to threats that he might decide to carry through with.

Before going to trial, Louise's attorney requested my father by legal order all the usual things such as: business records, sales of gasoline, insurance policies, income taxes records for the last 3 years, statements showing net worth, and I could go on, but I think you get the just of all of this! Many people were handed subpoenas from the cashier at the Savannah Bank and Trust Company to the American Oil Company. They were all directed to bring forward information about the dealings on the and off the record with my father.

Maybe Lila Bland! Love that name!

Even the other so-called women, Lila Bland, who it seems was also involved with daddy's rentals and businesses got a hand delivered subpoena! This order respectably required Ms. Bland to show proof of all deposits/withdrawals to all check and saving accounts between these years of 1941-1943. And any records showing any lock boxes or safety deposit boxes in your bank individually or doing business as Helmey's Filing Station or Helmey's Garage! I just loved the name Lila Bland!

After several jury trials resulting in two of the same verdicts, Lousie finally got a winning case, and it was made her case official. She got her alimony of $150.00 per month, which was deserved. And there is more, she also supposedly got a sum of $6,750.00! It all took place and was finalized in the year 1944!

In the year 1997, which I only found out about after reading all the legal stuff, he was sued for a cost of a living increase. I never knew about this year's lawsuit. Daddy just paid for it and moved on! I can only assume!

IN THE YEAR 1983 I KNEW ABOUT THIS LAWSUIT AND WAS VERY MUCH INVOLVED!

In September 1983 my father received official legal paperwork for the garnishment of funds due to Mrs. Louise Helmey! And that amount of $6,750.00 showed up again in the paperwork that was hand delivered to my father by the local sheriff!

At this time, my father was 83 years old, and his mind was slipping a bit. In other words, you wouldn't always get the same answer to the question asked. It had been 39 years since this divorce decree had been supposedly settled accepting for paying the month alimony. Over the prior years I watched as daddy either sent a check or signed the back of his social security check and mailed it off. To be honest, and since a lot was going on during this time, I wasn't keeping up with this. I just thought it was being taken care of.

So, I called up our lawyer Mr. Bergen to get some badly needed advice regarding my father's divorce of 39 years ago. And you must know it certainly was a strange thing that I was taking care of this, but this is what it took being my father's daughter! It was determined by the attorney that we needed to go through the process of answering the questions and sending the information back to her attorney.

Now believe me, I wasn't happy about this at all. A person that carries a grudge for 39 years and then treats it like it only happened yesterday really does have a problem. I would hate to think that for 39 years; all she thought about was getting back to my father. Now, don't get me wrong, I know daddy was very bad during 1943. However, taking everything this far, especially when I am now the one taking care of it, was just wrong!

While sitting with my attorney and discussing with him my options regarding my father's 1943 divorce decree. I had a question, and it went like this: What would happen if Daddy aka Judy did not do anything? What if daddy just cut off communications and let the attorneys talk? And talk they did!

134

IN 1985 THE END WAS NEAR!

So, here's how it went, we sent in the paperwork that was currently required to her attorney. Then I had daddy's attorney call her attorney so that he could pass on this profound message. My attorney told them that this would be the last time he would communicate with them. He had been fired, and it was decided by the defendant (my father, but really his daughter) that this chaos would stop here. In other words, "If you are going to have him arrested have at it! Yall, can take care of him!"

So therefore, not knowing what was going to happen next, these thoughts stayed with me for a while. And just like that I really forgot about it!

A BIG THANKS GOES OUT TO CINDI BUTTS FOR INTRODUCING ME TO CHAD DOVE!

I do not want to forget to thank Cindi Butts, my hairdresser and friend of many years! She introduced me to her friend Chad. And it is true what is said about Cindi, if you need something, I mean anything, you might want to ask her first before looking to hard. After all she knows the where's, the how's, and the who's! Heck, she might even be able to tell you about something even before it happens! So therefore, I guess you could say, and I will, Cindi doesn't just take care of my hair and is my friend, she keeps us in the KNOW!

Again, A big thanks you go out to Chad Dove for digging so deep and uncovering this information that I would have never known! And it's more official, my father was a rascal for sure!

In 2024, when I was finishing up this book, Chad Dove did a little checking into my father vintage court records. And boy, this stuff was pretty darn interesting. While reading through daddy's big pile of many divorce decrees, DUI's, assorted marriage licenses, details of my mother's car accident court drama, and lots more I found this piece of paper.

On March 4, 1985, by court order, my father's back alimony and monies due involving this case were dismissed! What did this tell me? They didn't want to take care of him either! Please know that I loved my father very much and did take care of him for many years, but sometimes a daughter got to do what a daughter got to do! In other words, play your cards just enough to win, but don't show your hand!

MULE POWERED TIMBER CARTS!

Back to yesteryear...My father's automobile repair shop was doing well. My father had devised many ways to make a car ride smoother on the bumpy roads. He always told me that the early cars rode like the old timey timber carts that were pulled by a team of mules. Back on the farm in his younger days my father's job was to load the timber cart with sweet potatoes and take them to the market. Once the cart was empty, he purchased lumber and took it back to the farm. So therefore, he really did know what a timber cart rode like! When I brought my first Chevrolet Stingray in 1974, he also said it rode just like a timber cart! Come to think about it, daddy never offered to try and make my car ride smoother, but I bet he could have for sure!

Felt Hats and Shoe Leather!

Way back when, there were a couple of techniques that my father came up with to smooth out the car's ride. According to the tale told, he used felt that hats were made of and old/new shoe leather. He placed a series of layers in the shocks and springs, which helped cushion the bumps. He even told me that General Motors used his idea in their shock system. According to my father he had all the business he could want! Car owners were happy to let him try his new and different ideas on their bumpy riding vehicles sometime referred by him as motorized timber carts.

He branched out and started selling used cars. It wasn't long before he had a wrecker service, too. After getting this up and running he started fixing wrecked cars. According to my father, since he knew all about cars it might as well capitalize on it. So therefore, he was involved in cars and all that it implied! At least for a while this is all he did!! However, then my father had a visitor...

Sherman I. Helmey. This picture was taken supposedly during Daddy's so called "Official Gangster Days!"

137

The story is about how my father met Big Al Capone!

HOW MY FATHER MET THE FAMOUS AL CAPONE

Over the years I have always told this story about my father and Big Al Capone keeping in mind that this information did come straight from the old horse's mouth. According to history Big Al was considered the worst gangster of his time. However, my father always told me that Big Al was nice enough to him. I always remarked, "Daddy Big Al could have most likely been linked to hundreds of deaths during his time!" Daddy would just laugh and always say, "He didn't kill all of those people by himself!" And then he would change the subject.

According to my father this happened one late afternoon at his shop, which was in historic downtown Savannah on State's Street. For those of you that know anything about downtown Savannah you will know the exact location when I say, "My father's shop was located next to Bradley Lock and Key!" The only thing that separated the two businesses was Bradley's vacant lot between the buildings.

It seems that my father was working late one night when a couple of guys dressed in old dirty overalls walked into his shop asking for a quick repair job. Upon accessing the damage, he found that their brand-new Ford truck had a slipping rear end differential. I always asked what this rear-ended thing was. And daddy always replied, "As time marched on, the rear end differential became known better as the guts that turns the wheels as well as things it was attached too!"

After a moment, daddy would say, "This new Ford truck was also leaking brake fluid too!" My father then suggested that the man take his new ford truck to dealership the next morning, because it had to still be under warranty.

TOP HATS, TUXEDOS AND BRAND-NEW SHINY BLACK PATENT LEATHER SHOES!

The owner then asked if daddy could fix it and he replied yes, but it's an 8-hour job. My father then told the owner that not only was it a lengthy repair it was also going to be very expensive. After hearing daddy's suggestion, he calmly asked my father to fix the truck and then to personally deliver it to The Desoto Hotel, which daddy replied, "Certainly!" The men in overalls paid Daddy with hundred-dollar bills. It was then that they asked if there was a place where they might change their clothes. Daddy pointed the way to the restroom, which was outside. Both men went on their way to change their clothes.

Before leaving one of men walked back into garage to get something out of the truck and it was then that Daddy noticed that the men had changed from old dirty overalls to top hats and tuxedos. To top their already smart outfit off, they were each wearing a brand-new pair of shiny black patent leather shoes!

After a couple of hours daddy went out to the garage to check on his mechanic's progress. Upon reaching the truck he realized it was unusually quiet. The closer he got to the truck the snoring got louder. His mechanic wasn't asleep, but in fact had passed out. The smell of liquor was very strong. Daddy scratched his head while wondering where the liquor had come from. Drinking was never allowed on the premises unless he was the one doing it.

He started looking at this truck that was packed full of all types of vegetables. Then he started thinking about the repairs and the damage to this new truck. It certainly wasn't unusual for a new truck to break down. Heck, they did that all the time. As he looked the truck over, he noticed that the tires either looked low or maybe the load was extra heavy. Then a light went off in his head, which got brighter the more he looked at the new truck and listened to his drunk worker let out yet another loud snore. He walked over and began removing some of the not so heavy vegetables. He found the real cargo that was hidden underneath all the vegetable baskets. At first my father nearly panicked, but after a few minutes he knew what he had to do. He would have to stay up all night, fix this truck, and then deliver it to the hotel as he had agreed.

SHOE SALESMAN CARS!

When he arrived at the Desoto Hotel, which was one of his own stomping grounds, he looked for the gentlemen. Upon finding one of them he held out his hand hoping to deliver the truck keys, but instead a handshake took place. He asked my father, "Do you know who I am?" My father replied, "I think so!" At that time the gentlemen introduced himself as Al Capone. According to my father it was at this time the deal was made. After a long conversation and I can only assume, knowing what I know, that Big Al just might have made my father an offer that he could not refuse.

My father's job regarding the Big Al era was certainly interesting. He was to pick up the trucks, bring them back to his shop, and then upgrade them as ordered. This boils down to making a truck that was surely overloaded not look so but still ride normal. My father-built compartments in unnoticeable places where cargo could not be seen. He even gave these cars and trucks a nickname. He called them "Shoe Salesman Cars."

Although this picture was taken at low tide and in the mid-eighties, you can see where once the tide floods how easily a loaded small wooden rowboat would be able to navigate through this area. (In our area we have a 6-to-8-foot tide every 6 hours.) This is the spot where the small boats made way to get to Greens to unload! My father always told me that timing and tide was always a problem. So, here's what those that picked the liquor up in the larger boats did with this so called "contraband" until tides were right.

How the liquor got where it was going!

Way back when, this would be your view if you were looking out one of the windows at Green's during a low tide stage! Don't you wish old wooden boats could talk? And if they did, what would they have to say!

Tides, Timing and No Excuses!

When the bigger boat or boats arrived at the coast smaller boats would head out and pick up the liquor. The larger boats would make way as close to shore as they could, way anchor, and wait to unload. Once again as I think about all this, I must wonder about sea conditions and small boats. This area is known for its rough conditions even at the calmest times. Since there were hardly any sort of navigation aids during this time those captains handling the boats were all navigating by the seat of their pants! And of course, I am sure if they didn't get the job done, they would have to deal with something far worse. According to my father there was this code, and he called it "no excuses!" The big guys in fancy suits and $100.00 shoes didn't care how the job got done much less ever consider sea conditions into the delivery factor. They wanted the liquor delivered at any cost and that was the bottom line.

So, here's how it was explained...

The larger boats would pick up the liquor from the ship, which was anchored offshore. These boats would then navigate as far as they could and unload their contents. Now here's where it gets interesting. I always loved this part of the story. According to my father platforms were built in the creek, which the larger boats offloaded the cases of liquor onto. Every time I ride through any of the small creeks at the back of Wilmington Island, I always look for old broken-off pilings. These pilings weren't left over from a dock that was built to go ashore. These pilings weren't placed near any land. They were placed in an area where the larger boats could get to no matter what the tide might be. This is where they would offload the liquor onto the platforms and head to unknown parts.

Here's yet another twist...

The captains on the boats were always taking what they called "their share." Even though they got paid for doing this job there was always some stealing going on. According to my father there was always a certain amount of taking that was allowed, but if you got caught…boy oh boy! Before the boats delivered the liquor to the platforms, they rendezvous to do a little horse trading. My father always said, "This is when a lot of heads turned so as to not see anything taking place." As you can see from this part of the story, there weren't any tally sheets of laden. And from what my father told me I am sure if there were they would have been tampered with too! So, as I listened then and now after thinking about it, I guess this was just the way it was.

Here are the leftover remnants of a liquor holding platform. After years and Years and years of deterioration some are in better shape than others. While navigating the back waterways as a small child I noticed that some platforms were larger than others. My father always said, "Each platform was built with the materials that they had on hand at the time." So therefore, I guess this is why some platforms were bigger than others! Just to give you an idea of how much tide rises and falls, this is a low tide picture. The dark line up in the marsh grass is about how high the water level gets to on flood tide.

After all the secret meetings took place, the boats would lay beside the platforms and stack on the cases of liquor. As soon as the tides were right the small wooden row boats would make way to the platforms to pick up the cases of liquor. Now for yet another twist to this tale… My father told me that the rowboat operators would then push off X number of cases of liquor right into the mud. After this, their plan would be to take the loaded cases of liquor to Greens and get unloaded through the secret trap door. As soon as their job was done, they would then row back out and pick up their cases of liquor out of the mud. In some cases where the mud was extra soft some of the liquor was never found. As a child I must tell you every time I ride by a broken off piling located in the back river, I think about stopping and digging to see what I might come up with.

THE TRAP DOOR REVEALED!

This is a picture of me (Captain Judy) standing over the trap door, which was located inconspicuously in the floor of "Greens!" The "Speak Easy" called Greens was located on the back of Wilmington Island.

It was built on the bank and its foundation extended out over the water. This room that had the trap door was located at the end of the building. It had its own entrance, which allowed the trucks to be able to back right up to it. This made loading procedures a lot easier, and it could be done without a lot of audience. My father told me that when they were bringing a large load of liquor to the back of the Island a big party was always planned.

Small wooden row boats could paddle right up under the building. Once underneath the contents of the vessels were unloaded and then loaded into the line of waiting cars or trucks. While all of this was going on there was a big noisy party going on in the main part of the building.

As a child I visited a friend that I went to elementary school with. She lived with her parents that owned the property that Greens was built on. At this time, I can't say whether her family had anything to do with the 1930's movement. All I know is that in the fifties we played around, under, and inside of Greens. People would come to purchase drinks, tackle, and there were even small cabins that the family rented outside of Greens. All I remember as a child is that there were a lot of wooden boats, parts of sunken wooden boats, and a room off to the end of the place that we loved to play in. After all it had its own door, it was isolated, and it was a great place to play "hide and seek!" All this time as a child I didn't know about the trap door being located where it was. Little did I know it had been nailed shut so that it couldn't be opened? However, in the eighties when I was notified by a dear friend that Greens was just about to be torn down, I ran over and took some pictures. It was at this time that we discovered where the trap door had been nailed shut. (And this is the area that I am kneeling over.)

There were other things that I remember as a child about Greens. It had a screen porch that went all the way across the back of the building. It was a lot of fun to play on and a great place to get away from those big biting mosquitoes and pesky gnats. In the main room was a large wooden bar, which had a cash register on top of it. The kind with large buttons and a side handle. Of course, even though we were not supposed to mess with it we did, and boy was it a lot of fun. Then there was this painting of a lady, which hung over the bar. According to some adults this painting was what made this a place for "men's eyes only!" The fact of the matter is, had someone not mentioned it I would have most likely never noticed it. In the daytime it was semi-covered and at night it was unveiled for all, at least those that were allowed to see her.

147

Michele Gillikin, Tybee Island, is showing us where the lady with the ample bosom hung. Her grandparents owned and operated Greens during its hay day times. At this time, I am not at liberty to say whether Michele's grandfather was involved! However, if he wasn't he sure missed his chance!

The Ample Bosom Era!

So therefore, being a kid and as most kids are when told not to do something we did do it. While no one was watching we pulled away the loose covering to see what was underneath. To all our amazements it really didn't show much or, at least, to a kid who didn't know much anyways.

So, we looked at the painting trying to decide what the fuss was all about. Since it had been at least 65 years, and I am all grown up I do believe the first thought that ran through my head was "she is fat!" And remembering what I still remember along with keeping up with the times this woman in this painting was a little on the heavy side having what I would have called ample bosoms. (If only, I would have known to say that!)

As a child I had seen paintings like this but couldn't know exactly where they were from. If I had to think about it now, I might have seen something like this in a museum. So therefore, since I think you have the "just of this matter" I will call this era "The ample bosom times!" The reason being is that that's exactly what I saw and remember now as an adult!!

This is a picture of a women most likely from this era. In this painting the woman is showing her bosom and not her butt. In the painting at Greens the bosom was shown, and the voluptuous butt was partially covered!

THE PLANNING THAT TOOK PLACE BEFORE, AFTER, AND DURING THE TIME THE LIQUOR WAS LOADED INTO THE TRUCKS.

Boy, if this loading ramp could talk. This is where daddy worked on his customers' cars and trucks.

According to him this invention in his shop helped a lot. Mechanics could work on the vehicles while standing up. This was way before lifts just picked the cars up so that the mechanics could walk under them to do their work.

The person in the right-hand corner of this picture is Charles Eden who worked on and off with my father for many years. This picture was found tucked in my baby book with this top portion cut out.

I wish I knew what was cut out of the picture!

My father was a
Colorful Coastal Character!

According to the stories told to me when it came to the supposedly illegal transportation of liquor my father was involved from the ocean to the lands that it butted up to it!

Over the years, if you have been keeping up with my "Little Miss Judy's Believe It or Not Stories" you most likely already know that my father was a Colorful Coastal Character for sure! I will try to sum up how he got this title. My father was married 8 times and never stopped dating. I used to say, allegedly worked for Big Al Capone as well as spent time with Fidel Castro.

However, The American Prohibition Museum took the word allegedly out and put in "Yes Daddy was a gangster and yes he did work for Big Al Capone!" According to his story daddy had lunch Fidel Castro in the early thirties at the old Desoto Hotel. He was man of many means; he could fix anything that had to do with cars and could just about get out of any situation that he was in.

My father was the type that knew what to say and when! He always dressed like a millionaire, smoked a big cigar, carried a big roll of money, and drove loud colorful cars with profound fins. My father always held the attentions of beautiful women especially those with a very spirited side. If there was an idea that he needed to come up with this would end up being called "his specialty."

For instance: If there was a big crowd in the bar and he needed to get through quick all he would say, "Wet paint coming through!" And according to my father with that being said "the crowds parted!"

Greens back in its heyday!

This is many years later at Greens. And it was right before they were going to remove what was left!

Here's what was taken care of before the transporting of the liquor began...

According to my father those involved would be notified and then they would tell those that needed to know. The people involved were to notify their contacts at the police department so that heads could be turned!

Believe me, according to my father a lot of people were involved in this movement. Those on the force not involved were either not on duty or sent to cover other areas of town.

Now here's where my father came in... He modified the cars and trucks either furnished by Big Al or the ones that he directly picked up.

Daddy then beefed up the vehicle support system so that they didn't look unusually loaded. Then it was decided to put white marks on the tires so that those not looking could turn their heads easier.

According to my father those policemen that weren't on the payroll normally would be sent to other areas of town to police. The routes that run from the island to the inland were set in stone. At least until something happened.

Back in these days, according to my father there were so many involved that it kind of made things run a whole lot smoother.

WRECKER SERVICE ON CALL!!

All wreckers' services involved would be on standby to keep the convoy moving. My father said, "Many times a truck or car would break down!" The wreckers standing by would pick up the broken-down vehicles, which were full to the brim with liquor to keep them moving to the destination point. From the way my father explained it to me it was lots of fun to be involved and not dangerous at all. However, since I was a child and my father hadn't gotten hurt, shot at, and hit, or been put in jail, the stories were told with a lighter persuasion.

OUT OF GAS OR JUST PLAIN STOLEN?!

As you know I have been writing about my father's great lifetime of experiences and accomplishments. In fact, until recently I thought I had heard them all straight from the horse's mouth, at least until I ran into Mr. Smith. According to Mr. Smith my father employed him at the age of 14. The year was 1945 and young Smith was better known to everyone as just "A T." According to the story he said he would ride his bicycle to work every day. In a conversation with him I found out some new information and stories that I hadn't heard from the horse's mouth (straight from old Dad) After I share a few with you I am sure you are going to understand probably why good old dad didn't tell his sweet innocent daughter these true tales.

Mr. Smith shared this one story right off with me. It came out of his mouth as if it happened yesterday not over 50 years ago. According to the story, my father had a new car stolen from his place of business. The police, of whom were very good friends with Daddy, received the missing report of the car and were doing everything they could to find it. In the early forties my father had another big boat which I didn't know about. The boat was docked at what is known now as "Thunderbolt

Marina" Daddy hadn't purchased his place on the river as of this time. The story could go in many directions, so I will try to stay focused. My father was working on his boat when "young A T" came running down to the dock screaming that the police had found his stolen car. They wanted him to come right at this moment to claim it. My father jumped up, ran up the dock, got in his car, which was already manned with a driver that went by the name of "Slick." When they arrived at the destination point, they found that daddy's car was still intact. In fact, all they had to do was to put gas in it and drive it home. (Sounds fishy to me) All while this was happening back at the boat, it was sinking. Daddy left the dock hose running in the boat.

Here's Pete and my father better known during these times as "MOOSE!" The apartment that Daddy also known as Moose, Mr. Helmey, Captain Helmey, and later as daddy is behind the wall that the clock is mounted on. According to my information, daddy had two homes, the apartment, and the boat.

HIS BOAT!

In one of my many stories I had written about my father accidentally sinking his large boat. He did in fact leave the dock hose water running in the boat while he left on a more hurried quest. After he finished taking care of his quest (another story) daddy returned to the dock to find only the top of his boat showing. This was because it had sunk as it was tied to the dock.

I heard about this boat through an old employee of my father that worked for him during the mid-forties. Some of the stories that he shared with me were ones that I had never heard before. So therefore, this information that I am sharing with you is second hand, but maybe better than the firsthand information that I got straight from my father. According to the story the boat that sunk was wooden; but it wasn't a "Miss Jerry" boat. All my father boats before my mother's era were called "His boat!" This was before my mother entered the picture. It didn't have a name and according to the story daddy just called it **"his boat."** When he wasn't living in the apartment above his used car lot, he was staying on the boat, which was considered his second home. My father spent a lot of time going out on the town, smoking cigars, drinking liquor, and chasing women. The gentlemen that I talked to never said anything about daddy doing labor of any kind. He was more like a diplomat. His job was to take certain people out, show them a good time, and then reap the benefits. Among some of his guests there could have been the mayor, chief of police, etc. I think you get my drift. At any rate, he would be out late and when he woke up, he was either hung over or worn out from all his nighttime work. My informant told me that my father had a remedy for his morning problem. He would take a gallon jug of water, lift it to his mouth, and drink it until he could hold no more. At this time his stomach looked as though it was going to explode, but luckily it didn't. My father would wait a second, then exhaled all the fluids and whatever else was left over from the night before right where he was standing. (This act in my world would later be called "Purging Daddy's Way!")

156

After this act, he smiled, and said, "Let's go, it's another day, and time to make another dollar!"

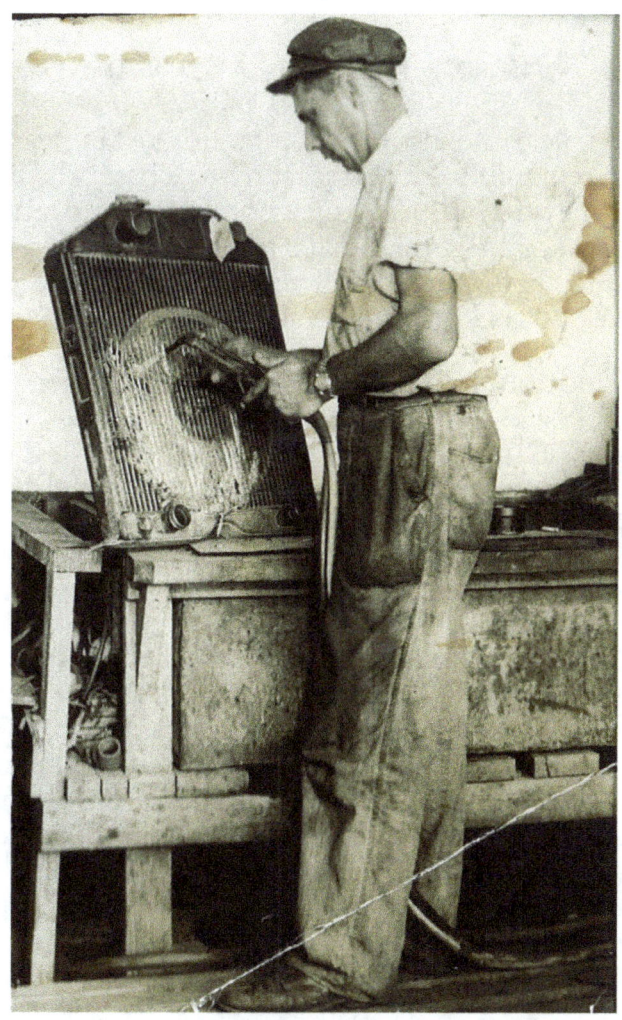

The old hunting accident strikes again!

Jack Graham, nicknamed Daddy Jack, is working on a radiator that was removed from a car, which had been shot or should I say shot at during a hunting accident. Now that last sentence has more meaning than you think, and it really makes absolutely no sense. Let me explain…First hunting accidents meant there was a shootout between either the police and the bad guys or the bad guys and some more bad guys. The rules as well as the law that tried to keep these guys straight were all jaded at best.

Mules, Trucks, and Cars

During the forties he also had a most interesting career in the automobile repair industry. At least that's what I was told. Upon meeting my new friend, "AT" of whom worked for my father in the mid-forties, things might have been a little different. I knew that daddy repaired and fixed wrecked cars, but he never told me about his **"wrecker business!"**

After thinking about it I guess he needed a wrecker to bring in the damaged cars. My thoughts were that he just hired some other business to take care of that. I was very wrong. My father had one of the biggest wreckers' services in Savannah. He could haul everything from a **"Mule Carts to Large Trucks!"** My new source "AT" never mentioned what they did with the mules. I must ask that question when I meet with him again.

At any rate, according to "AT" (one of my father's trusted employees of the mid-forties) the wrecker business was handled a little differently back in the good old days. When a wreck was reported, an officer was sent to the scene, and it was up to him to contact the wrecker service. In other words, it was his choice. According to the story back in the old days those companies that paid the most got the "most wrecked car calls." I had to wonder how the police called the wrecker service. After all cell phones weren't invented at this time.

I then found out that the larger wrecker services had short wave radios right in the shop. Back in the old days you could hear all conversations. The police's frequency was out there for everyone to listen to, and they did. Payment for calls and tips came in the form of clothes, liquor, and just plain money. However, I feel that there were other things that were offered, but I don't think "AT" wanted to share them with me. (Now is the time to use your imagination!)

After hearing this story, I wonder if anything in that particular business world has changed?"

Re-conditioned Tires!

I have known Wilton "Wil" Denmark for many years. The fact of the matter is that I consider him part of my family. As we talked just the other night, I found out yet another almost lost chapter in my father's already interesting life. According to Wil, his Uncle Roscoe and my father were somewhat friends as well as business associates. Wil's uncle got things done for certain people and my father during this time was involved with the selling of so-called "fine used cars."

Wil's Uncle Roscoe was a master of many trades, which we can talk about now without fear of being summons to the courthouse as a possible witness to so called "city crimes." His uncle pretty much would have fallen into the same possible line up as my father did. This boils down to the fact that we can't say for sure, because they didn't get caught much less charged for any of these so-called illegal activities that they "were or were not" involved in. Boy, now that was a mouth full, but I think you now get the just of it!

As a child it was Wil's job to run errands for his uncle, which his pay was turned into some extra spending money. He never questioned what he was told to do. Uncle Roscoe told him that my father was in bad need of some tires. Wil's first thought right off was his uncle wasn't in the tire business. As I said earlier, he never questioned, he just listened. So, here's how it played out. Wil collected tires from anywhere, delivered them to daddy's car lot, and received a sum of $.50 cents for each one.

I don't know about you, but when I need tires, I just purchase them at the store. However, the tires that Wil picked up weren't new tires, but rather real used ones. Back in the old days there was a shortage of everything so therefore "old stuff was used to its up most!" Wil would look for tires that were just plain discarded, even if they had holes and badly worn tread. He would even remove tires off abandoned cars. He also told me that the cars that remained in one spot too long might also become shoeless. Most of the tires were then re-conditioned and re-used. I guess

159

I had best explain re-conditioned from this standpoint. They weren't re-capped, meaning adding more rubber they were just re-conditioned!

According to Wil, all tires were given new tubes, mounted on rims, filled with air, and attached to daddy's machine, which turn them slowly. While they were turning a laved/blade of sorts would cut the worn tire groves deeper making the tires look newer as well as thicker. Thus, you now have my father's meaning of "tire re-conditioning!" After the grooves were set, they were painted black!

I learned a few more things, which wouldn't have been funny then, but surely are now. According to Wil, all used cars that had any sort of "link slippage" had some unusual additions. Instructions were given and followed out. Wil's job was to stuff banana peels into the gearbox. This made the gearbox seemly tight sending the message of an "automobile that doesn't have that many miles!" When Wil got to the part about the weight of the oil that was put in the old transmission, I thought I had better stop here

Wilton Rahn Denmark (1936-2018) and Captain Kathy Brown!
Now, here are two people that made a great pair not only in friendship, but
also in business! From the fruit to the carpentry business these two were like
"Hammers and Vidalia onions!"

1960's Era!
Three ladies, four bottle and two cans!

Many, many, many years ago Brenda, Susie, and I were a Trio drinking team! It looks like we could have made a commercial for a beer, champagne, or cola! Now I don't think we were really drinking those so-called alcoholic drinks. I believe we were using them as props, but I really can't say for sure! Why? We were a happy trio!

THE INTERNATIONAL ORDER OF HOO-HOO

Many years ago, as a small child, I used to spend a lot of time at my uncle's dock house, which was located on Turner Creek. I remembered the framed so-called letter that had a black cat circled on top of the page, which was hanging on the wall in the kitchen. On this page was a list of nine rules for my uncle's club.

This is me, Captain Judy Helmey and my now world-famous Uncle Bobby's (also known as "Reds Helmey") gift to me. He had saved the actual framed rules of his father's club. As he handed it to me, I knew that now I could find out exactly what the real rules back then really were... and you are not going to believe this story although it's oh so very true! (As all are!)

As a child I never read the information, I just assumed what it was all about. I always thought it was all about my uncle's club stating the "dos and don'ts." I assumed rules like "couldn't cheat at the poker game, which meant you can't get caught cheating!" At least that what's my father always said! Another thing I thought probably was listed was that "some attendees cooked *while others cleaned up!*"

Now you must know as a child I didn't make this stuff up, I lived it! You know the old saying, "if you want to really know the truth ask a child!" As I got older my thoughts and reasoning behind what was on this framed page changed. They got more realistic. For instance, still not having read it, was the fact that "Wives couldn't attend, only girlfriends" were allowed at the meetings. Heck, as I got even older, I knew my earlier thoughts were right. Children were not allowed at the dock house after dark!

One day while swimming in my uncle's wonderful homemade saltwater swimming pool I overheard the adults talking about suggesting that some sort of lighting or a handrail might be needed on the long walkway to the dock. As I overheard this, I looked down the dock and even though I had walked the "Very long and narrow" I never thought about it needing lights. However, as I mentioned earlier, "children weren't allowed after dark!" Apparently, someone had fallen off the dock in the dark and not only was it hard finding him or her, but it was also very uncomfortable trying to get them out of the marsh. Since my father had fallen off our dock, which had rails on many occasions, this statement didn't shock me at all. Not only that, but I certainly didn't think that the addition of handrails or anything else would help their problem of falling into the marsh! After all, if you are going to fall "then fall you are!"

As I am writing this, I can still remember the dock house, the swimming pool, and the outhouse, which was located inside. Before I close this paragraph, I must tell you about the toilet room, also known as the inside outhouse. The toilet was basically a toilet seat on a wooden box. A flushing handle wasn't needed because the box had no bottom. The bottom line to the toilet was what you deposited fell through the open bottom and right into the water. The cool thing was this: When it was high tide, the currents took whatever dropped out quickly away as if it never happened. However, if it was low tide "all deposited things just dropped into the mud!" This meant the children could go see as many times as they could what was stuck in the mud. I remember on many occasions 4 or 5 of us children standing over the box and peering down below. The descriptions shared especially by those that didn't do the dropping, was to say the least "priceless!"

My now world-famous Uncle Bobby also known as "Reds Helmey" brought a gift to me. He had saved the actual framed rules of his father's club. As he handed it to me, I knew that now I could find out exactly what the real rules back then really were... and you are not going to believe this story although it's oh so very true! (As all are!)

I really need to share with you my version of my Uncle Bobby's story from the start to the present. And I think I will, with his permission, "do just that!"

Just to raise the bar of interest, here is a little teaser into "Reds" life. On one occasion just to wish his wife happy birthday, he rented a plane and pilot, put on a parachute, jumped out of the plane, and made a crash landing on top of their house. He only broke both legs, but he healed completely!

My Uncle was the first to "high jack a plane to Cuba, once landed got abducted on purpose was seriously interrogated, live through it all, escaped back to the US, and never once spent any time in jail! Just these stories about the capture and what he did to survive are so interesting that I share them with my fishing customers all the time.

They must be good, because they hang on to every word and always want to ask questions to which I always have some sort of answer! And there are lots, lots, and lots more! But as usual I had better get back to the story at hand!

Big Time HOO HOO's

Photo from Reggie Goldsmith

WHO are these fine-looking businessmen? I will give you a hint, back in the day they were members in "good standing" with the HOO HOO'S Society! They all worked in the same type of business, played the same kind of cards, tried to meet at least once a month in a secret place, and of course made some very serious decisions! It has been said on more than one occasion that decisions made by the HOO HOOS altered as well as changed a lot of paths even while in mid-stream. This picture was taken on August 16, 1960, at a HOO HOO's meeting at a secret as well as secure location.

Front sitting: (left to right) Cecil Walling – Dixie Lumber Company (owner Chas. Mikell) Ralph Sterling-Savannah Planning Mill (owner Mac Helmey Captain Judy's real uncle, not a cousin)

166

Back row: (left to right) First businessman don't know name, Tommy Shearouse (owner Shearouse Lumber Company) Billy Jones (Savannah Lumber & Supply) and Reggie Goldsmith (U.S. Plywood Corporation) Boy, these were some big HOO HOO'S!!

My good friend Reggie Goldsmith back in the good old days was a member in good standing with the fraternal order of Lumbermen HOO HOO Society. To sum up the HOO HOO Society from my prospective I would have to say, an interesting group of businessmen who shared the same interest meeting together so that their beliefs in the lumberman's society were sustained. And of course, this society had its own Code of Ethics! There was a total of nine codes of ethics. I will share with you my favorites: Only members could attend unless prior approval was made beforehand. No cheating was allowed while playing cards, (that would have been unethical) and if you drank too many HOO HOO beverages you had to stay overnight.

This is a long time gone picture of my uncle Mac's dock house aka Secret HOO HOO meeting place. The dock's walkway to the house was very long and had no handrails on either side.

This is the walkway that led up to my Uncle Mac's dock house. The rails started right as you reached the dock house. At the end of the stationary dock was a floating dock! The crabbing was great both catching and cooking!

And here's a picture showing part of the rail-less walkway back to the bank. From the picture you can see how long a walk it was to get back to the bank. If you had consumed too many alcoholic beverages causing you to wobble, then you most likely would have fallen into the marsh. And there were many walkers that became or were professional rollers in the mud!

This last rule was especially true when the secret meeting was held at my uncle Mac's dock house. The reason a member had to stay due to too much consumption was because of the long dock walk back to their car. To get to my Uncle Mac's dock house was like taking a long hike. The walkway wasn't too narrow, but the absence of rails created a big problem. If you happened to wobble you might just fall off the dock walkway, which puts you landing right into the muddy marsh. Now I am not going to say, "I saw this happen!" I am going to say, "I heard about it and the conversation went some like this...when we finally found him, he was laid out in the marsh and snoring up a storm!" And it took us forever to get him out of the mud and back onto the walkway! Not only that, but he was also a muddy mess!!! And I will leave the story with that last line!

My HOO HOO friend for life Reggie Goldsmith

Reggie honored me with this great award "Historian for Life of the Savannah Order of Hoo-Hoo!" After receiving this award, it made me more aware of my duties regarding HOO HOO's. So, here's my job: Captain Judy's Code of Ethics Spread the word about the HOO HOO's and to find others!

Reggie Goldsmith holding my award and me (Captain Judy Helmey) holding framed "HOO HOO" Code of Ethics (Which is the award that my Uncle Mac received Tuesday September 15, 1964, for all his grand service while he served as president of Savannah HOO HOO Club #134!)

Now find out how the numbers behind the names started... Here's what I found on the web about how the HOO HOO organization got started in the first place!

History does seem to repeat itself...My Uncle Mac also received an award from the HOO HOO'S.

On Tuesday September 15, 1964, my uncle, Mr. Mac Helmey was given an award for doing such a fine job as president of the Savannah HOO HOO Club 134.

My uncle was presented with a framed copy of HOO HOO Code of Ethics.

170

*Friedman's Art Store did a great job of framing
this historical piece of HOO HOO history!*

Which was signed on the back.

To Mac Helmey

With assurance of our highest esteem and with grateful
appreciation for your splendid service as president of Savannah
HOO HOO Club number 134

(Sorry for any misspelled names)

(Please know the back of the frame is worn and the pencil in
handwriting has faded. Some of the names might be spelled
wrong from my end.

Also, if anyone knows any of these persons, please contact me
912 897 4921 or by email fishjudy2@aol.com)

Gertell Leo 53926 State Deputy Snark, Clarence A. William, club past president 55880, Ralph G Stisberry past president 61770, Wall 53930, last name S. Hanul past president 59831, Durrant 58052, Henry S. S...th 58058, Lester R. Shearouse 59830. Those that signed with no membership numbers: George B. Waits George Whalley Jr, H Cliff Stubley Jr, Chuck Hanul, Fred L. Shearouse 63816, Dorothy Williams, Peggy Sterling, Ruth Waite, Freda Helmey, (Uncle Mac's wife), Mrs. Shearouse, Jan Daniel (there were other names, but couldn't read the writing)

The HOO HOO History!

HOO HOO degrees Team of Ohio Cira 1930

Founded in 1892, the Concatenated Order of Hoo-Hoo is a fraternal organization of lumbermen and those in trades related to the lumber industry. Hoo-Hoo is the oldest industrial fraternal organization in the United States. At the height of the organization's popularity, membership totaled more than 13,000. The headquarters of the order and its museum are in Gurdon (Clark County), the town where HOO-HOO originated. The order had more than 3,500 members in 2004.

The order was established on January 21, 1892, when six men saw a need for an organization to promote unity and fellowship among lumbermen and to combat a possible split brought on by the lumbermen's broad range of pursuits. These six men— Bolling Arthur Johnson, a journalist of Timberman in Chicago; George Washington Schwarz of Vandalia Railroad in St. Louis; William Starr Mitchell of the Arkansas Democrat, Eddy Barns of the St. Louis Lumberman; George Kimball Smith, secretary of Southern Lumber Manufacturers' Association; and Ludolph O. D. Adalbert Strauss of the Malvern Lumber Company— began discussing the idea of an organization for lumbermen.

In Hotel Hall in Gurdon, the men set up the basic tenets of the order. Hoo-Hoo was to be an organization comprising men with high ideas, and the order's motto became "Health, Happiness, and Long Life." The group (led by Johnson) decided that the board of directors would be called the "Supreme Nine." The names of the directors were: Snark of the Universe (president), Bojum (chaplain), Scrivenoter (secretary), Gurdon (sergeant-at-arms), Senior Hoo-Hoo, Junior Hoo-Hoo, Custocacian, Arcanoper, and Bandersnatch (later changed to Jabberwock). Some of these names were derived from Lewis Carroll's Hunting of the Snark, which one of the founders had recently read. The name "HOO-HOO" also had a unique origin. In Kansas City, about a month before the founding of the order, Johnson had used the term "HOO- HOO" to refer to an unusual tuft of hair on the head of Charles McCarer. McCarer became the first Snark of the Universe and was given number one membership.

And here's the thing some of you might not find this so significant but think about it. This started with a few lumbermen that got together with an idea, formed a secret club, had nicknames based on a cat's 9 lives, staged meetings in all the right places, and controlled pricing of lumber with a wave of the hand. And they had fun doing it! What does all this boil down too? Worldwide Lumber Mafia Club with a serious plan!

No Helmey can ever go to Cuba!

Not going to Cuba!

A friend of mine, after hearing my story about never being able to visit Cuba, brought me this fine Cuban Cigar!

So now for those who don't know the whole story let me explain...

My father did some mechanical design work for Big Al Capone during the thirties. In other words, he built trucks that hauled the liquor. My father also spent some time with Fidel Castro! At this point, if I was born or if my father wanted to visit Cuba it most likely would have been a very pleasant trip. My father spent time with Fidel in the now famous Desoto Hotel, located in beautiful downtown Savannah, Georgia. According to my father the new hotel and the old hotel had zero in common. Apparently, it was the best meeting place at the time. My father had lunch with Fidel and according to the story fresh raw chicken was served.

As soon as I heard this, I quickly turned up my nose, but then my father quickly said, "I ate steak!" Now for the rest of the story...

In 1969 my father's nephew high jacked United Airlines Flight 459 from Savannah, Georgia, made it land at the Cuban airport, and had the pilot to broadcast over the radio that Big Red was coming to kill Castro! As soon as the plane landed, he was taken into custody and thrown into jail. From Jail he went to interrogation, and then into prison. According to my cousin, Reds Helmey, things were bad! After hearing all the things he had experienced I couldn't help but share with you this most unbelievable story. Please remember all my stories are based on things that really did happen. As I have said many times "They are just too good for me to have made up!"

My cousin had red hair, and it seems that in Cuba this constitutes a religious foe-pa. (Not the right spelling, it's another Judy-ism!) This boiled down too; those that had red hair weren't just simply strange crazy, they were possessed, and if you killed them bad things would happen directly to you. However, there wasn't anything mentioned in these beliefs about torture, so there was plenty of that to go around. After the Cubans got tired of torturing or half killing Reds, he was then thrown back into the dark damp prison cell.

This is just about when the Reds decided to start acting in the part! Before departing the US, he had studied the Cuban's religious culture, so he was fully prepared to act the part of a red headed incarcerated possessed individual! So, at night he would get down on all fours and start howling at the moon. And after he got some attention, he then would pour from his pants cuffs his kept stash of ripped/bitten off finger and toenails. You see every time his nails got long enough, he would cut them off and keep them. I know all of this sounds crazy, but oh so true. After getting all the nails piled together, he would toss them up and let them fall on the ground. Then he would act like he was studying them while acting out the message sent. According to Reds it wasn't long before the guards had a most standoffish attitude toward him.

It was decided by someone that that Reds should be shipped off to Russia. Somehow, someway, the Reds escaped and got back to the good of USA! Once arriving here of course, he was arrested for high jacking a plane. But here's thing, he was never really locked up in jail and according to sources that knew that Reds was sent there on a mission by the CIA! To this day, I don't know exactly what that mission was. However, anyone with Helmey anywhere in their name shouldn't, couldn't, and ought not to visit Cuba, because it might just turn into a one-way trip! Believe me, they do not forget! Those powers in Cuba harbor all considered wrongdoing to their country. However, if you stay away, it might never come up! So therefore, we Helmey's are staying PUT on USA soil!

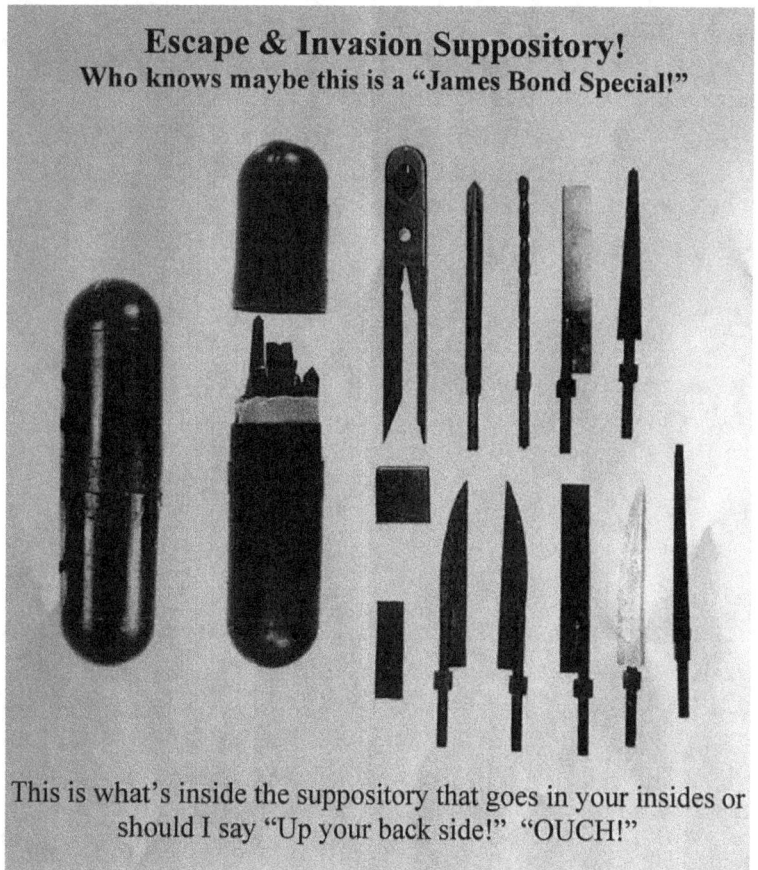

Escape & Invasion Suppository!
Who knows maybe this is a "James Bond Special!"

This is what's inside the suppository that goes in your insides or should I say "Up your back side!" "OUCH!"

Back in the sixties this was some of the secret stuff that the CIA supposedly used. As the writing on the picture indicates, this escape and invasion suppository does in fact slip into your insides through the back side. (This is a better way of saying large tool kit is inserted up your rectum!) And I would have to agree that a big OUCH would most likely be involved.

So, the mystery is basically solved as to how my Uncle Reds escaped from the Cubans. From the looks of what was inside the suppository tool kit he was the one with the advantage. So therefore, it is official he pinched, cut, sawed, drilled, dug, ply, file, and fought his way out!

Before you go to thinking that this was a made-up item in my head read this...The international Spy Museum in Washington, DC has a rectal tool kit on display. It is a tightly sealed, pill shaped container full of tools that could aid an escape from various sticky situations. This neat gadget was issued to CIA operatives during the height of the Cold War. After reading all of this I summed it all up by saying, "It's a weapon that is kept down under, which once removed and properly used can get you out of a lot of bad situations!

https://www.atlasobscura.com/articles/cia-issued-rectal-tool-kit (I just wanted you to know where this information came from)

The new and improved Desposito's restaurant re-opened in 2023. On any given visit, you might find this information on your place mat. According to this story, my cousin, Reds, planned this attempted assassination of Castro while eating in the original Desposito's in January 1969!

One ham sandwich to go!

And I must add that the Reds came by our house the night before the high jacking took place. My father and uncle's Bobby took off to the dock and was down there for quite a while. When the back door opened, they both walked in, and my father told me to fix Bobby a ham sandwich. I jumped up and started making a sandwich that none of us knew that we would be talking about for a long time! As soon as my father told me to fix the sandwich, he said, "Your cousin needs to eat something before he leaves!"

After what happened, happened I often wondered if my father knew beforehand that Bobby was going to high jack a plane to Cuba! And I also remember that Uncle Bobby had a big bandage on his head. He told me that a wooden block/tackle had come loose at the lumber mill and swung down hitting him on the head. I must remember to ask him next time I see him if that injury was real or not!

SKYJACKER IN SAVANNAH:
THE MURDER PLOT AT DESPOSITO'S

In January of 1969, United Airlines Flight 459 from Jacksonville, Florida to Maimi made a scheduled stop in Savannah, Georgia. Thirty-six year old Army veteran and former Green Beret Robert Helmey, who many know as "Red", was aboard the second leg of that flight – but not as a passenger.

Helmey, who lived and worked in Savannah, was known to suffer from delusions after his tenure in the military. And around the time of Flight 459, he believed he was a key operative in an FBI-CIA mission to assassinate Fidel Castro.

It's said that Helmey planned his assassination attempt at Desposito's Seafood Restaurant just outside of Savannah on the Wilmington River, with staff and guests of the no-frills seafood shack non the wiser that a skyjacker was plotting amongst them.

On January 11, Helmey enacted his plan and hijacked Flight 459 with a .38-caliber pistol, demanding that the plane be rerouted to Havana, Cuba with the message, "Tell Fidel, Red is coming."

Upon landing in Havana, Helmey was imprisoned for 109 days, but was released and acquitted on the grounds of temporary insanity. He later shared his experience in a book, The Lemon Dance: Tell Fidel El Rojo Is Coming, and is happy to sign autographed copies in Savannah today.

The first photo is of Bobby Helmey aka "Reds "giving a class on "Demolitions Reconnaissance," to a group of Special Forces "Green Berets," at West Point in 1967.

My uncle Bobby aka "Reds" with his finest of covert friends!

The second is an A-Team; L to R: 1st person, Lt. Charlie Lee, second is Lt. Curtis Harper, 3rd is Sgt. Leo Woodcock, 4th is Sgt. Reds Helmey and fifth is a covert operative Big John Wayne, who was not supposed to be in photo, but he was. The Photo was taken one month before Cuba on December 11, 1969! I certainly do wish I had been there to hear this conversation!

RUBY WAX SHOW

Interviewing some of Savannah's most unusual Coastal Characters!

Who is Ruby Wax? She was a very nice lady, wonderful, easy to talk to too, pretty, and funny as heck! Prefect for this job! Ruby is a British American actress, comedian, writer, television personality and mental health campaigner.

Ms. Ruby Wax and Uncle Bobby "Reds" Helmey Hijacker Extraordinaire While riding on the Miss Judy Too Ms. Ruby interviewed Uncle Bobby! We were just-a-cruising on the beautiful Wilmington River!

During the mid-nineties, while visiting Savannah, Ruby Wax sought out to interview a few of the most unusual coastal characters. Among those picked were Crazy Jack Gilmore, Bobby "Reds" Helmey, Lady Chablis, and then I was added to the mix Captain Judy Helmey!

The plan: I was to take Bobby "REDS" Helmey (my uncle) Crazy Jack Gilmore, Ruby Wax, and her team for a boat ride. And during this time, I was supposed to simulate catching fish, which is very hard to do when you only have 30 minutes. (But we did our best) Ruby held the rod and Uncle Bobby pulled on the hook end so that it looked like she was fighting a very big angry fish!

For bait we were using my father's favorite for all kinds of reasons. It was called "The Hoochie Coochie Tuna Fire Tail! To be honest, I don't think anyone who watched the show knew the difference, since we lost the so-called fish before it landed!

After the fishing/boat riding trip, we all met at McDonough's bar in downtown Savannah to do a little karaoke. Lady Chablis "The Doll!" would be joining us. And we were all going to try to sing Midnight Train in Georgia!

To be honest, it was a great show, and I hope you all can see it for sure! It was taped on VHS, and thanks to Eric Darling "eThree Media" I have a digital copy!

Captain Ali Young and Captain Judy Helmey, when were so very young! We were singing Midnight Train in Georgia! Thank goodness Ali's great singing voice made up for my out of tune vocal cords!

My Uncle Bobby aka Reds Helmey and one of his best friends from yesteryears Crazy Jack Gilmore 1933-2021

Uncle Bobby aka REDS told me this "DNA Test or Not!"

I must share this bit of information with you. After all, if I don't you won't know. So here goes. While we were filming the Ruby Wax show, my uncle Bobby and I had an interesting conversation. I will never forget this as long as I live. If you have been reading my writings, you already know that my family is not like most. Or I should say, "I don't mind sharing information about our family that should normally only stay in the closet!" I have a theory about all this interesting family unrest, and it goes like this. If I don't tell you what I know it might as well not have happened in the first place! And it is my belief that everyone should feel this way!

So, here's what Uncle Bobby aka REDS said, "Judy it is possible that I might be your brother, because your father bedded my mother during my conception time. Or since my supposed father is your father's brother, I might be your cousin. However, I could be your father, because I slept with your mother during the early fifties!" We both decided that it is what it is and left it at that, meaning No DNA Test needed!

The conversation with my Uncle Bobby and Ruby Wax just got better and better. She asked him, "How were you supposed to kill Castro?" and this is what Uncle Bobby said, "He was carrying a ring with poison that would kill once he touched Castro!" Then I listened as he told Ruby that he never saw Castor. So, the ring, which was incased in a suppository, which was inserted up his rectum was never used. However, as you already know the other things in the suppository such as tool were used to escape!

My uncle Bobby never served anytime regarding this hijacking. When he went to court, he took the insanity plea. Doctors determined that Uncle Bobby had Transitory Delusional Psychosis. Now that is a mouth full of words! What does this mean? It is a type of mental condition where a person can't tell what's real from what imagined!

The bottom line and as you already know my uncle was not delusional during this time, he was on the government clock! And thank goodness we can finally talk about it! I must drop Ms. Ruby Wax an update!

1934 Hudson Terraplane "A bootlegger's haul butt car!"
"Buck Jones's rocket and the church door"

Here's a story that I certainly do think that you will enjoy reading. My father's brother had a son which I called Uncle Bobby. Back in the old days you had cousins that fell under the categories of 1st, 2nd and 3rd. Bobby fell somewhere between the 2nd and 3rd bracket. However, I always have and still call him "Uncle Bobby."

Uncle Bobby spent a lot of time with my father, who he called Uncle Sherman during the thirties. In fact, he had one fond memory that happened in 1938 that he wanted to share. According to his story, Bobby was around six-year-old when this happened.

Take it away Uncle Bobby...

Uncle Sherman's Garage on State Street had a ramp on the second floor that allowed him to drive cars up and down. The area upstairs was used to repair and do other (secret) things to automobiles. Every time my dad took me there, I would ask uncle if I could ride up the ramp.

This day, Uncle Sherman said, "OK." The ride up was very uneventful, but the rocket ride down will always be remembered. After Uncle Sherman gunned the engine of the big Huston "Terraplane" automobile at the top of the ramp, he dropped the clutch and away we went. In those days, brakes didn't always work the way they were supposed to, and this day was no exception. We exited the ramp at a high rate of speed onto State Street. On the opposite side of the street was the "Lutheran Church of the Ascension." Things happened fast, but I do remember Uncle Sherman saying, "Hold on, Bobby, I think we're going to open a new door to the church!" I don't know how he was able to make that turn without flipping the car over, but he did. I guess the LORD didn't want a new door added to the church or maybe he was just looking out for us that day. Oh yea! For those who are too young to remember-Buck Jones was the first man to ride a rocket ship to the moon - at least that's what happen in the "Chapter pictures" at the Savannah Theater every week in 1938. You can be proud of your dad. He wasn't perfect, but who is... his generation is a dying breed. They didn't know the word "I can't." He had "True Grit."

And then Captain Judy says, There are a few things that I would like to say about this fantastic almost forgotten story. Knowing my father with that big cigar that he always smoked I bet the sparks were flying. According to my father the Huston "Terraplane" was one of most famous 4-door cars ever made. It became known as "A bootlegger's haul butt car!" I certainly do wish that I had been there to experience this escapade." Thank you so much Uncle Bobby!

Now for the update about Cousin Reds aka Uncle Bobby…

In the summer of 2023, my uncle bobby aka Cousin Reds now age 92 stopped by for a short visit. He looked great for sure! We sat around under the bait house shed and talked about old times! And as quickly as he arrived, he decided to depart. However, as he was getting into his car, he said, "I got them out alive!" I perked up, and asked, "Are you talking about Cuba?" and he replied, "Yes!"

After all these years, we finally get a little information of exactly what happened regarding good old uncle bobby high jacking a commercial airliner and making it land in Cuba. First, please take a strong look at my uncle Bobby, does he look crazy? I don't think so! Now, according to the news published, back then, once home, in the courtroom, my uncle was acquitted on the grounds of temporary insanity!

Ok, now that I got all of that out of the way. However, the story has a lot more backbone. It seems that my uncle really was a real time key operative in an FBI-CIA mission to assassinate Fidel Castro. All this certainly does make good sense, he was qualified, had information that no normal person could acquire, a successful working plan to infiltrate, and the knowledge as well as the tools to evacuate when it was time!

As if all of this isn't enough proof there actually was an official mission that of course no one has ever been able to talk about, but just so you know, the goal was accomplished!

Who is this? This is my mother Jerry Lovett Helmey (1925-1957) she is sitting on the end of our dock, which is still located on Turner's Creek. What can I say about this picture? I believe the metal tub was called a number three wash tub. Anyhow, this is what my father called it. I know as a child it was used for dock baths for me and to carry ice to the boats. Behind my mother pulled up on the bluff is a wooden rowboat. This is where we would pull our small row boats, turn them over, paint them with red antifouling paint, and then put them back in the water. Now if the row boats were going to remain on the hill for any length of time... we then turned them back over and filled them with water. Why? The water would keep the boat's boards from shrinking!

Little Captain Judy Lynn Helmey dressed for
success and sitting pretty for the camera man!
Photo taken by Olin Mills Studios.

Now I can't say for sure who dressed me, but I have a good idea. This outfit looks like I was dressed by those wonderful ladies at "Punch and Judy's" Back in the fifties there was a child's clothing store located on Broughton Street called "Punch and Judy's!"

Their main entrance faced Broughton Street in what is better known now as historic downtown Savannah. Punch and Judy's also had a back door entrance with a buzzer button! You could drive straight up to either drop the child that you wanted dressed off and/or to pick up those that are already dressed. I would be that child. This was an interesting place for sure. They were known for catering to many parents. I loved this place and knew everyone that worked there. My father purchased a lot of my clothes at this store.

His other favorite place to shop for my clothing, which he brought by the cases was Kahn and Company. This wholesale house was located on West Broad Street, which is better known at this time as Martin Luther King Boulevard. For those that are scratching their heads this wholesale shop was right next to the old Cranman's Sporting Goods Store. Now, neither of these places, I am sad to say, "Are not still in operation!" However, their buildings are still holding strong and have been refurbished back to the "old school looks" by SCAD! When I happen to drive by these old locations it starts me to think about the good old days! Daddy and I would park in the back lot behind Kahn & Company! Or sometimes we would park in the Cranman's side parking lot and shop in both places!

Clothing brought by the cases mean some interesting things. Instead of 3 to 4 pairs of socks or underwear there were dozens of them. Instead of picking out a color there were either all white or multiple colors. Daddy brought all our towels, sheets, and bedspreads in the case. When it was time for me to wear training bras, yes you guessed he brought them by the case. To be honest, I grew out of them before I used the 24 training bras that I had in my dresser drawer.

PURPLE TREE LOUNGE AT THE MANGER HOTEL

Once my father dropped me off at Punch and Judy's he would head over to the Manager Hotel to have a drink at the Purple Tree Lounge. After a few cocktails, he would drive down the alley behind the store, hit the bell, and they would bring me out. I loved it when daddy went to the Purple Tree Lounge. The reason being is he would always bring me the stir sticks. Believe me these were the most unusual stir sticks ever. The sticks were purple, yellow, and brown. They were shaped like a tree that had lost its leaves. Now that I think about it, they were also very dangerous. I really don't know how daddy didn't get his eye poked every time he took a drink. However, after thinking about it I bet that this is why he took them out first! Boy, it sure is funny what you remember as a child!!

My father was quite a fisherman in the daytime, and he was also an avid night person. In fact, I spent many great times with him on his nighttime rendezvous. These outings were great, especially for a child who was only about 8 years old. Just about every outing had the potential to turn into an adventure. For instance the times that we spent at the lounge located in the

Manger Hotel.. If you are a long time local, you must remember this bar in the hotel it was called the "Purple Tree Lounge." It was so neat, especially for an eight-year-old. When they brought Daddy and I our drinks both drinks had a tree stir stick in it.

This was the good times before business owners feared people poking their eyes out with sharp objects. This stir stick was neat. Daddy would always give me his. I would stick my cherries on the limbs of the trees. It sounds like this story is about purple tree stir sticks, but it's not. It's more about the fish tank that was in the "Purple Tree Lounge." Their large aquarium had lots of small to large goldfish swimming around in it. As I watched the fish swim, I noticed something different about them. You could see their insides functioning as the fish moved about. It was even weirder when they turned the lights down. The fish became illuminated with their bodies becoming lighter than their insides. You really could see everything that was going on inside their little bodies. I watched the food go in and the food go out. Now that I think about it, I had no idea what daddy was doing all this time! All I could figure was that he was missing a great fish show that was so very interesting!

BUSTER BROWN SHOE STORE

My shoes always came from Buster Brown's, also located on Broughton Street. All I remember about this shoe store is that they had child size wooden animals for us to sit on. They had a giraffe, horse, lamb, and a cow. As I can remember the colors of these animals were anything, but natural. They were painted all sorts of colors. And to top off this craziness they had different colored dots and squares painted all over them.

According to my father, shoes with leather needed a little "set up" before wearing them. He always took his sharp knife and cut grooves on the bottom of my shoes. The reason being and it was a simple one… I needed as much traction as I could get when trying to make way!!

I can't say who cut my hair, but I have a good idea. There was this barber shop and I think you know where I am going from here…Yes daddy took me to his barber to get my hair cut. There I said it!

As a child I loved getting a brand-new pair of shoes. I loved to take a trip to Buster Brown's Shoe Store. When we arrived the shoe salesman would sit in front of me and put my foot on a cold metal made foot-measuring device. He always asked me to stand up, because according to him when doing so my foot would be longer! As a child I never understood that statement.

At any rate, I would put my foot on the cold metal foot measurer. Upon me doing this he would measure both the length and push this slide to the ball of my foot to access the width. All of this for a pair of shoes! This was the part I didn't like. I just wanted a pair of new shoes not an examination of sorts. Daddy always let me pick out the shoes that I wanted. Believe me at this time "topsiders" weren't on my mind. However, "black and white oxfords" were. For me this was a two-tone shoe that had lots of possibilities. When I first wore them, they were black and white meaning free of all scuffs. After a few weeks the white part matched the black part more and more. After a month or so I could take daddy's black shoe polish or his black spray paint and end up with a solid black pair of shoes. This is where I usually got in some major trouble. One time I forgot to take my shoes off when polishing them, which meant my white socks were ruined. The other time I forgot to put the black spray paint that I used back on his boat. My father was mad about the white socks, but when he couldn't change the color of that lure he was pulling, the screaming really began!

This is a picture of the painting that still hangs in the family home and brings many wonderful memories!

ONE HORSEPOWER!
RUNS ON CARROTS AND APPLES!

Polly Wylly is the rider, and Laura Connerat is on the skis. And they said it couldn't be done. Well, it could, it would, and it did! And here's the proof! Who needs a Johnson or an Evinrude outboard when you have one solid serious horsepower!

I just love going to Ace Hardware located on Wilmington Island! When I do, I never know what I might put in my shopping cart. On this day I ran into a friend from yesteryear Polly Wylly Cooper. And a grand conversation we had for sure. Since we ran into each other at the pet section we started talking about our wonderful pets. Ms. Polly started talking about her horse of many years ago. It seems back in the sixties everyone had a horse that lived on Savannah Beach. And Ms. Polly and her friend were no different, they wanted a horse too!

According to the story they decided to look for a horse and they started this quest with the abattoir, which was located on Louisville Road. Once finding the horse of choice and maybe the only one there at the time they asked the price. The abattoir wanted $35.00 for the horse. Why? Because that is exactly what he would get paid after he turned the horse into the ingredients for dog food.

So, Ms. Polly and her friend Laura had to come up with some cash quick. So, this is what they did...They started gathering up stuff that they thought the butcher might take in trade for the horse. They loaded up the car with a pair of hunting boots, an empty birdcage, and a slightly used pair of stilts. Along with these items they had also baked him a cake and they had $12.00 in cold hard cash! According to Ms. Polly the deal was sealed without hesitation. And just like they became owners and saviors of a malnourished one-eyed horse, which they immediately named Cyclops!

And with that being said, "Here's the short story written by information shared by Polly Wylly Cooper!" And you are going to love it!

In 1956, best friends Laura Connerat and Polly Wylly rescued a one-eyed horse later named Cyclops from the abattoir on Louisville Road. They took him to Tybee and fattened him up! Here's Cyclops pulling Laura on skis in the Back River with Polly in the saddle.

TYBEE TALES AND TAILS
BY POLLY WYLLY COOPER

Years ago, children kept goats from Goat Island, ponies and baby alligators as pets. Dogs chased sand-crabs on the beach and swam out to fetch sticks thrown into the river by their owners.

Nothing, however, was more thrilling than an early morning bareback gallop along the hard sand at low tide. Jumping into the foaming breakers on a frisky horse was beyond exciting.

But the best of all...yes, the *very best*...was water skiing behind a horse cantering along the water's edge on the Back River.

That is exactly what happened in the 1960s. Best buddies, Laura Connerat (Lawton) and Polly Wylly (Cooper) rescued a pitiful old horse from the glue factory on Louisville Road, transported her to Tybee, named it Cyclops, and proceeded to fatten her up!

Cyclops lived in a big pasture owned by the Strongs at the north end were Kay Strong kept Queenie, her dappled gray mare. Willie Whalen was nearby with his small ponies called Marsh Tackies. Today the pasture is a campground with rows of RVs.

Water skiing behind a horse!! What? Impossible! No, not at all.

The girls saddled Cyclops; Laura slipped on her skis and sat down in shallow water; Polly climbed aboard. Trotting at first, then cantering, Cyclops easily pulled Laura up on the skis until she was skimming along the surface.

Seeing this spectacle, sunbathers rolled up their towels and fled for the dunes as the trio sped by. There is only one old photograph to prove this really happened. An artist was commissioned to paint this scene from the photo.

Cyclops lived three more years being brushed by Tybee children and fed sweet oats and hay - a happy ending to this tale. Please know that Polly Wylly Cooper was nice enough to write this story and to share it with us!

Now we can all read this great feeling wonderful story repeatedly forever and never forget the star, Cyclops!

I published this story after the passing of my long-time friend Kitty Strozier. Kitty was a seasoned resident of Tybee Island, Georgia. She had a wonderful soul! Believe me, time flies much too fast and I think of her often!

GREAT FRIENDS GOING FISHING!

This picture can only be named, "Having Fishing Fun!"

My father with his famous cap and King Edward cigar, Captain Sherman I. Helmey, (1901-1993) Captain Chuck Fischer (1945-2016) Wilmington Island, and me Captain Judy Helmey at the helm! And yep, that's Kitty Strozier (1946-2016) Tybee Island who owned and lived in Stiff Kitty's Cottage for a long as I can remember! Don't you just love Kitty's expression? It basically says it all! No matter where Kitty was her presence was known and in a grand way too! (Stiff Kitty's was the name of her Tybee Island cottage, which was located behind old MacElwee's Seafood Restaurant!)

LITTLE FISHING FEET

My good friend Kitty loved to go deep-sea fishing. Back in the real old days I would have what we called "the girls yearly fishing trip!" We would load the old Miss Judy boat up with so much stuff that her water line would temporarily be changed for the day. Bag after bag was brought onboard as if we were going for days rather than just for the usual 12 to 14 hours. At any rate, after the loading took place, we pushed off!

Everyone was always on time because they all knew that the fish were waiting for us! We hadn't pushed off good before everyone on board was talking about who was going to catch the biggest fish. As our arrival time at the fishing grounds got closer the bets and the previous fish landings got bigger. This just goes to show you a fish no matter whether it is in the water swimming or not the tales still do grow! And that is why fishing is so much fun! Not knowing of what you are going to catch and how big that sucker just might be!

I remember this one trip where Kitty was sitting on the gunnels of the boat with her rod in one hand and was holding on with the other one. It was a little rough that day, but it didn't matter to us seasoned fishermen. The day was about over, we had caught quite a few fish, but no big ones to speak of. However, we still had at least another good hour of fishing left before we had to head in. I looked back just in time to see Kitty basically fall off her present perch and onto the deck where she landed. A little drinking and wave action might have been involved!

Her rod was still in her hand and the laughing was quite loud. As Kitty began to stand up, she felt a large pull on her line. Apparently when her feet slipped out from under her she fell a "hookset was installed." For those of you that don't know Kitty had very little feet, which meant for balance, especially on the boat, she danced a lot to keep from falling. Well, in the case of having a big fish on and the boat also rocking her feet were doing overtime in the moving/dancing department. Kitty was rocking, dancing, and smiling big as she reeled her large catch to the boat. We watched it knowing that this was probably going to be the biggest fish of the day. As Kitty reeled, anticipation raged!

Back in the old days I don't ever remember carrying a dip net as we do this day and time. It's probably a good thing, especially in Kitty's case. The large gag grouper was not only the catch of the day but also of the year. This all boils down to the fact that Kitty's fish wouldn't have fit in the net anyway. With a large smile on her face, that I can still remember today, and those feet that would hardly keep her balanced, Kitty held the big grouper up dancing all the way! No music needed! I don't have to tell you about the ride home, because you can already figure out how that went. To this day I don't know whether the fish hit or her own move while trying to adjust those tidy feet caused the great memorable fall. However, the bottom line to this whole story is that "sometimes when you fall there is a catch!"

This is Kitty Strozier and one of her most interesting pets. Meet Dewberry! Dewberry went everywhere with Kitty! And heck you might not see him, why? Because he was always in Kitty's purse along with her camera and her X-ACTO knives! And this was far before dogs were accepted like humans! However, Dewberry was a sincere exception!

Dedicated to my friend Kitty Strozier
February 6, 1949-January 9, 2006

Cape Cod and Kitty

I must tell this story about my good friend Kitty Strozier. About 40 plus years ago Kitty and I visited Cape Cod on a fact-finding mission. Kitty being an artist and I being a fisherman we both decided that this was a perfect spot to visit. After having a very long nervous plane ride we landed and started making our plans. During this particular time the movie "Jaws" had just arrived in the theaters. It was the talk of the town. We thought more so, because most of the movie had been filmed on location where we were visiting. So therefore, we decided to take time out to go see what all the fuss was about. After viewing this movie, I started looking in certain places that held water long before I sat down and definitely where I intended to swim. This vacation turned out to be a memorable one for sure! Heck, I still am talking about it!

Boat in the background of this picture!

For those of you that remember Captain Emmitt Bridges (our neighbor) the boat in the background is the Glenda-Jane! He named it after his only daughter and wife. I used to laugh at Mr. Bridges! Why? Most of the time when he would get home after a day of offshore fishing, he would have so many fish that they would be lying all over the deck and engine cover! To this day, when I see him on the dock, I always tell him I caught my fish out of his fishing hole! And we laugh together because we both remember the loran coordinates! What are they? 61073/45345 you notice I left the tenths of micro-seconds out!

KITTY'S DAY ON THE OCEAN...

Shortly after returning home some friends of Kitty's chartered my boat. Kitty was to be my first mate so off we went. About four hours into the fishing trip, we hooked something that was so big that it made the poor old reel sizzle! The fish took most of the line off the reel I had to quickly put the boat in reverse to keep the line from being snapped. As I said, "it was a big fish!" The angler was reeling, the fish was swimming, and the reel was trying. All hands and heads were hanging over the gunnels in hopes of seeing this big monster fish. For two hours the fish fought us. I can say this "excitements were high!" After the big fish slowed a bit and I backed off to make more of an impact on the fish. Soon after that the big fish was brought along side, we gaffed and brought it onboard. It turned out to be a fish that I hadn't seen much of in my young "at the time" fishing career. It was an amberjack that weighed well over 100 pounds. Had I known at the time I would have most likely sent the paperwork in. However, none of us even thought about it.

Kitty Strozier leaning over a big 100 pound amberjack!

We were all big eyed about the whole thing. Kitty was so excited. I can still remember the expression on her face to this very day. She said, "All I could think about was where the fish was dragging us and what it was going to do when it was done taking us where it was going!" I never told Kitty that I had the boat in reverse! Now you know how much the movie "Jaws" impacted my very good friend Kitty!"

An oldie but a goody! This is Kitty Strozier February 6, 1949-January 9, 2006! Her life was cut short, but memories of Kitty will certainly live on!

KITTY STROZIER TITANIC ERA

Kitty loved to fish, and she did it as often as she could. Not only that, but when she did "fish were favorable and most often bite her hook!" Kitty by trade was an artist, but not like most. She could draw or paint a picture of you that looked just like someone had taken it with a camera. Her talents didn't stop here she was great in coming up with "super ideas in the brainstorming department!" I'm talking about great selling ideas! She worked for many years with Big Time Longwater Advertising Company owned and operated by Powerhouse Elaine Longwater. So, as the reader you should know that Kitty was a shaker and mover in her field of expertise!

Back in the old days we all thought that Kitty studied obsessively the ins and outs of the sinking of the great Titanic, because she certainly did know a lot about this famous incident. It seemed to be one of her favorite past time hobbies! The fact of the matter is on one of her bookshelves she had a completed model of the Titanic. It was detailed for sure! Another one of her many accomplishments!

If you have ever visited Stiff Kitty's house it was lined with deck chair types that came directly from the "Titanic Era." In fact, when she sat in them, she looked almost too comfortable. As time passed, I noticed that Kitty knew a lot or maybe way too much about this famous sinking. As she supposedly did her research, many, including myself thought that a lot of the information that she shared wasn't found in any of those old, published accounts. Kitty, even remarked while laughing, "That she might have actually been there in a previous life!" I hope that she gets to go back and revisit those special places from the past that were always on her mind. If there is such an opportunity once we do leave this world I certainly hope, especially in Kitty's case, that things go pretty much like they did in the latest produced Titanic Movie. That her ending is the beginning of great adventures to places that she might have already visited! **Dedicated to my friend Kitty Strozier February 6, 1949-January 9, 2006**

Skiing history was made by our own Sue Carter Miss Savannah 1967!

Sue Carter crowned Miss Savannah 1967

Somewhere between July and August 1967 I was contacted and asked if I would teach the current Miss Savannah how to ski! At the time, I was working at the Savannah Inn as a water ski instructor. Some might know the hotel on Wilmington Island as the Sheraton. Then there are some alders that might say "Oglethorpe Hotell!" I guess you could say, "I am one of those alders!"

Anyhow my job was to sit around the pool and wait for potential customers. The hotel would book them, send them directly to the pool, and off we would go. The hotel's pool was located right in front of the dock. I would drive to work in my boat, tie up at the hotel's dock, and then walk to the pool. I guess you could say the pool was my office! And of course, while I was waiting, I could swim. And they had a great high dive, which I loved! Their snack bar made the best juicy real time hamburgers and potato fries. Boy, I would love to be able to make an order right now!

208

If my customers happen to be children, the parents just dropped them off. I especially remember that most parents, at least the fathers, were always dressed in the finest flashy business suit types and expensive shoes. Most of their shoes had pointed toes! I always looked to see if there happened to be any bulkiness on the right or left side of the sports coats. Even if I could not tell whether one was packing, I always presumed there was a piece hidden somewhere somehow! My father was the one that started me looking for the signs. It was kind of a game with us!

Most of the time I had some good young water skiers! Then there were times where we did more dragging than skiing. When trying to learn to ski was more trouble and stopped being fun we then tried a little old fashion tubing, which is not a thing like today's! Tubing wasn't popular because the tube we pulled was a real black tire tube. We pulled regular and tractor size tire tubes. But here's the thing, that hole in the middle would always mess you up! So therefore tubing, at least in the sixties, just wasn't that much fun. So, we did more sitting in the tubes in the water than pulling them behind a boat!

As children we all loved to hang in our inner tubes in the creek. We found that with a little foot sideways paddling we could make the tube carry us round and round. It was plain good fun laying our heads on the tube while circling and drifting from one dock to another. The fact of the matter is that sometimes we did this for so long that it made some of us a little nauseated. I don't know if you did this as a child, but I used to love twirling around and around in the yard until I fell on the ground! Now here's this thing if I were to try this now I most likely would fall possibly breaking something, get vertigo causing me to lose my balance for a few hours, and heck I might even throw up! Getting old is not for sissies! I find myself saying this all the time!

Anyhow, after planning with the person in charge of hiring a ski instructor for Miss Savannah, plans to meet were arranged! As soon as Sue Carter aka Miss Savannah arrived, we immediately hit it off. The reason for the urgently Sue was supposed to ski with the five Florida girls that were water-skiing their way to Canada's EXPO 67. Five ladies were on a 2,500-mile water ski expedition from St Pete to Montreal Canada for a visit to the EXPO. Miss Savannah was skiing with them in the waterway near Isle of Hope. Heck, this was a big deal!

Water-Skiers Stir Up Splash

Five "ski-daddlers" from St. Petersburg, Fla., stirred up a splash in Chatham County Sunday.

The quintet, all blondes, are on a 2,500-mile water-ski expedition from St. Pete to Montreal, Canada, for a visit to Expo 67.

They pulled into Brady's Boat Works docks, accompanied by Miss Savannah, Sue Carter, Sunday afternoon to the ogling of some 200 spectators.

The girls are Linda Austin, 15, Cathy Austin, 12, Mary Fras, 23, Patricia Markus, 27, and Alice Roberts, 21.

They're being towed by a 40-foot houseboat.

The appearance here was sponsored by the Visitor and Convention Dept. of the Savannah Area Chamber of Commerce.

When the big day arrived, from Isle of Hope to Thunderbolt spectators were numerous. Those of us that had boats got the best view. And since I was supposed to pick Miss Savannah up when the skiing show was over, I had Carte Blanche! We got to see everything up close!

I guess I should tell you how Sue aka Miss Savannah did when it came to skiing. Well, I truly believe Sue already knew how to ski and that she only needed a refresher course, which I gladly helped her with. Sue did quite well with getting up on skis and handling her balance! After I thought about it, I think refresher course was so that she had a less chance of falling and then there was the hair! We couldn't get that wet! How did it all turn out? Sue Carter aka Miss Savannah did a great job of representing Savannah! She made us all proud! Sue skied with the ladies in a fashionable design and disembarked with perfect precise timing!

FLORIDA GIRLS WATER-SKIING THEIR WAY TO CANADA'S EXPO 67
Miss Savannah, Sue Carter, Joins Skiers at Isle of Hope as Expo Flag Flutters

I felt honored to be asked to be part of this skiing history! And for me being able to put these memories to paper for others to read is simply amazing! The best news is that after all these years Sue, aka Miss Savannah 1967, still talks and sends emails occasionally! Upon request she was able to send me this yesteryear newspaper article. Can she still ski? Heck yeah! And now you know the rest of the story!

SAVANNAH AREA OUTLOOK

Miss Savannah, 1967 Sue Carter (C) along with two of the skiers and Jim Gray project director.

211

Captain Alli DeYoung, Captain Kathy Brown, and Captain Judy Helmey

Soon to be Captain Alli DeYoung, Captain Kathy Brown, and Captain Judy Helmey. Little Allie dressed up like me for Halloween! I must say, "Alli did a great job of leaving out the wrinkles!"

Texas A&M College Graduate!

Update: Our Captain Alli DeYoung has graduated with HONORS from Texas A&M College! Her credentials and qualifications reach further than most dare to accomplish! We are now saluting her! And here the thing, if you are in the ocean, a big ship goes by and keeps blowing her horn, it just might be our Captain Alli at the helm!

HALLOWEEN 1958 STYLE

My father always took me out for Halloween so that I could collect my annual brown bag of candy. I always dressed up and it was a lot of fun. I tried everything from homemade costumes to store-bought ones. They all seemed to do the trick. However, there is one store bought costume that I will never forget. My father saw a cat costume and he brought it home. I was about 7 years old at the time, so therefore dressing up like a cat wasn't such a bad idea, at least until daddy made certain alterations to the costume. The tail of the cat costume simply just hung there. Daddy checked it out and found that he could stuff my tail with some of the white so-called cotton that he used for caulking repairs on his wooden boats. I didn't care all I was thinking about was all the candy that I was going to get and how much I could eat in one night.

After stuffing the tail with the so-called cotton, it created a bigger problem. The tail was too heavy, so it just fell to the ground. Now I had a cattail that was three dimensional, but it wouldn't stand on its own. I could tell that Daddy was in a mood or maybe he had a few too many cocktails. Now he broke the fishing line. His plan was to tie one end to the tail and the other end to the back of my costume, which he did in a fast fashion. I now had a state-of-the-art moving cattail that swayed with my walk. (Remember the lion's tail in the Wizard of Oz) I was ready to go "Trick a Treating" in my now daddy designer store bought costume.

Our first stop was great! I got lots of compliments on my costumes and plenty of candy. I really made a haul. Daddy even got a beverage to go. As the evening went on my brown bag got heavier. According to Daddy my "Trick a Treating" was just about over. This wasn't good news, but heck I was a little tired from all the walking with my tail swaying. We must have visited at least 10 houses. Our last stop had the noise of a barking dog in the background. I was a little afraid of dogs, since one of our neighbor's dogs had bitten me once before. I approached the door with caution. The dog was really barking at this point.

When the door opened, I saw the dog, which didn't appear to be that large, but it sure had a big mouth. Somehow after the owner told me that the dog didn't bite it escaped heading right for me. (I'm sure I looked like a small deer in the headlights!) Of course, I did what any seven-year-old dressed like a cat would do I ran with tail swinging in tow. The dog lunged and became attached to my tail. This, as you can imagine, slowed me down a bit. I could see my father running toward me, but it seemed as though he was in slow motion. At this point the tail ripped off, but unfortunately the fishing line didn't break. So now I had the latched dog in tow. Things couldn't get much worse. I had dropped my brown bag and now had a dog attached to my tail. I finally met up with my father and he immediately picked me up leaving the small dog still hanging. The dog owner apologized as he removed the dog from my tail. The rest of the story was easily figured out, so we went home. However, the candy haul for this house was unbelievable. I guess the bottom line is that you pay for what you get. In this case a little entertainment goes a long way.

The moral of this story is a simple one. "So-called cotton was made to stuff only into the cracks of wooden boats and fishing line is made for fishing not so for tail tying. Any alterations can certainly change the course of an evening."

No Trick or No Tricks,
Just some Darn Good Exotic Can Goods!

Breakfast of Champions! Captain Kathy is holding up her most special breakfast of all time, which after you read the story below, will better be known as her exotic foods!

Way back in the good old days while on the pickle isle in Lester Claxton's Wilmington Island grocery store The Piggly Wiggly I was approached by an older woman. She asked, "Are you Captain Sherman Helmey's child?" I replied, "Yes!."

And then she said, "I have a funny story to tell you! While I was taking my grandchildren's Trick a Treating last night, I stopped by your father's house to let my grands knock on his door. Your father answered with a smile on his face. I could tell he was complimenting the children on their costumes.

I watched Captain Helmey carefully dropped candy in their bags. I heard them thank him and watched as they came down the steps with their heavy bags. Heck, I thought, what did Captain

Helmey give them? Must have been a lot of candy? Well, as it turned out your father didn't have any candy. Apparently, he had eaten it or forgotten to purchase it.

However, my grandchildren did not walk away empty handed. As soon as they got back to the car, they showed me their unusual haul while sporting big smiles. He had dropped 2 cans of Vienna sausage and sardines in each bag. Since the kids weren't ever allowed to eat such stuff, this gift was as popular as candy! Heck, one child remarked, it's exotic food. Now, where in the world they got that word from I will never know! And I just wanted you to know that your father was a hit with my grandchildren!"

I am so happy that her grands got the good stuff, because I had already been told by another lady that her children had gotten a can of corn and stewed tomatoes. The fact of the matter is she was serving corn and tomatoes for dinner! Now you know for sure that Halloween wasn't just about getting dressed up at my house, it meant much much more! So therefore, if you run out of candy, just open your kitchen cabinets, and pick out some exotic canned goods! Because we already know from past experiences this can work to someone's advantage! Happy Halloween Always!

Happy Halloween!

Can't say for sure who exactly this is!

Maybe straight from the movie Wicked!

Rumor has it that she made an illegal landing at Savannah Hilton Head Airport, parked her broom, and everyone is looking for her!

I made a copy of this picture, which I took of the one hanging in the Wilmington Island post office!

If you see her or know her possible whereabouts, please contact the Federal Bureau of Investigation! (FBI)

CAPTAIN HELMEY'S YOUTH IN A BOTTLE!

During the seventies in his early seventies my father got sick and was hospitalized for about two weeks. I watched as his hair color went from very dark to lighter and lighter! As it grew longer it seemed whiter and whiter! It was truly a snow-white color. I almost didn't recognize my own father. Heck, he looked years older than he really was! This is when I found out about my father's "white hair-keep away concoction."

Apparently generously applying Grecian formula multiple times was his big secret to keeping his hair dark. And here's the thing my father always had a butch haircut, which means there wasn't much hair to color any way. However, the difference from not much white hair to not much dark hair was astounding. As far as I was concerned, I would keep his secret, and he could use this stuff until the cows came home!

So, I decided to ask my friend Captain Steve "Triple Trouble" Howell to do a little web surfing and bring me up to speed regarding Grecian Formula! He is very good at searching for this! The new, now more improved Grecian formula does not work, at least not like the old formula which really did work! And here's why... because the US food and drug administration deemed it necessary to require them to remove the so-called harmful lead acetate as an ingredient in the Grecian formula!

But here's the thing my father lived to the ripe old age of 93-years-old. He was married eight times and divorced 7 times! My father drank a fifth of liquor almost every evening before he left the house! He sometime mixed his

218

liquor with milk, because according to him, it made it a healthier drink. He never started drinking before 5 PM. According to him if you do, you just might have a drinking problem. He smoked a big King Edward Cigar but never inhaled! My father danced like Fred Astaire while wearing his side tied blue suede shoes! He always said, "All women loved him whether they knew it or not!"

According to my father he had a special magnetic form of CHARISMA! Believe me, from what I know; no one would argue this point, because it was oh so true! All this with the original Grecian Formula onboard four days a week! It seems there are a lot of people that have their own personal secrets, remedies and ideas when it comes to holding onto their youth! What's yours?

Parent's Logic

As a small child I always wanted a pony, but my father would never buy me one. It wasn't because we didn't have enough room, because we in fact had horse stables right on the property. His main reason for not letting me have a pony was because as he always said, "I would get run over by all of the traffic." Boy, if he wanted to see traffic he ought to see it now. Back in the fifties on the Island where I was raised there wasn't much traffic. So therefore, I decided to do my own traffic count. In the mind of a seven-year-old it sounded like a good idea. I decided to lie in the road and count cars. I must have lain there for a good hour before the car finally came by. Heck, I could have fallen asleep. At any rate, after I felt that my experiment was concluded I decided to go and tell daddy. I knew that he would be very proud of me. It turns out that daddy wasn't so proud of me. In fact, I was put on restriction for laying in the stupid no traffic road.

Well, this is me (Captain Judy with my captain's cap on) trying to climb a tree. My friend is my neighbor Michael Dunford! The photo was taken in my back yard. If the picture was taken further to the left, you would have been able to see the horse stables. Of course, my father would never let me have a pony or a horse even though we did have a place to put them! I was not happy about this!

When I wanted to go horseback riding, he took me out to my Aunt Hattie's farm, which was located on ever-busy highway 17. You must remember back in those old days' superhighway I-95 hadn't even been thought of. As I got older, I figured out that daddy either didn't want to take care of a pony or he thought I would get tired of one! He held steadfast with his decision, and I never got my pony.

However, I had a boat from the time that I was five years old! I guess according to my father, drowning wasn't an option in my case. However, getting run over by the one car per hour that passed by our house was. I will never understand a parent's logic!

The Helmey Clan was tailgating way before it became popular!

From left to right: My father Captain Sherman Helmey, his older brother Randall Helmey (Randall's wife Mamie, and my father's younger brother Mac Helmey! Here's a short recap: My father was married eight times and never stopped dating. Randall and Mamie were married for 60 years plus and only dated each other. Mac Helmey was married to Frieda for many years. Randall always told me that the reason he was the smallest was because his brother Sherman made him do all the work! The truth of the matter is my father and Uncle Mac on one hot summer day when the brothers were very young suggested something to Randall! What was that? Well, there was this rattlesnake in a ditch. The brothers told Randall, "I bet you can't jump over that snake!" Well, Randall made the leap, in midair the rattler jumped up and bit him, which altered his childhood greatly! Now you know the rest of this story!

A Thanksgiving Story:
My Aunt Hattie's Brown Bag Theory

My Aunt Hattie, who was my father's older sister, always cooked the best Thanksgiving dinner! Her cooking abilities were unbelievable. She would cook along with the help of Bertha doing almost everything from scratch. Aunt Hattie's Thanksgiving dinners took days to prepare. In fact, during my younger years, if I'm not mistaken, all ingredients including the bird were raised or grown on her big farm. However, the fruit that she used to make that unbelievable ambrosia was probably purchased from a stand right out there on Highway 17. I know that the pecans that went into this dish were picked from the farm, because quite often I helped with the gathering.

Bertha of whom worked with my aunt for a long as I can remember was always there to help with the "Thanksgiving Cooking Bonanza." I was always interested in how they made everything look and taste so good. Her personally grown vegetables were always the "perfect vegetable color." They baked a coconut cake that was 6 tears high. It never leaned or anything. The bad news is I wasn't always around for mixing the cake because this is one bowl I would have loved to lick. However, my aunt had this kitchen utensil that I later called a "child cheater." This reason was a simple one. Whenever I happened to be around when baking she used this utensil, and it would remove almost all the tasty ingredients from the walls of the mixing bowl. There was always a little left, which was only enough to get a short taste.

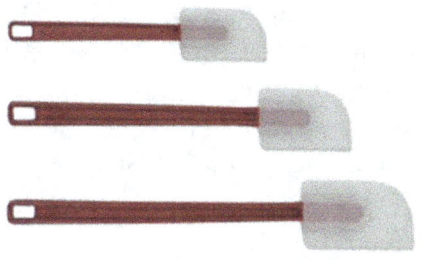

Child Cheater
also referred to as a rubber spatula

223

The turkey was always browned to perfection. Her secret was certainly one of a kind, at least in my book. She cooked the turkey in a brown grocery bag. The bird was put in the bag much like you would have put one in a state of the art "plastic browning in bag." The drums always stuck out a little, but not enough to let them be exposed to direct heat. There was another weird cooking method that Aunt Hattie used, which I am still scratching my head about! The turkey was wrapped in a sort of gauze that pretty much look like a bandage. When the bird was cooked and un-wrapped it also came out golden brown with skin and everything. However, when it was first put in the oven it looked like a real bona-fide "turkey mummy."

The food wasn't the only highlight of Thanksgiving Day. My Aunt Hattie always set the prettiest dinner table I had ever seen. She would always use her best china and silverware for this special occasion. The Table was huge. It would seat at least 12 guests. There were high back chairs with big arms rests. When you sat in them you knew for a fact that you had to be someone special just to be invited. The good news about my Aunt Hattie was that my father and I were always invited. It was a family tradition to spend Thanksgiving Day at her house. This dinner was always served at 2:00PM sharp. You could tell when dinnertime was approaching because everyone would start showing up. My father and I always arrived early so that we could all watch the televised New York Thanksgiving Parade. It was, as I said, part of a family tradition.

When it came time to eat everyone was gathered for a prayer. As a small child, I am sorry to admit, I always opened my eyes just to watch what every else was doing. Most of the adults were standing very still with their eyes closed. However, all of us kids basically did the same thing, watched and semi-listened to what seemed to be the longest prayer ever said in the world. At least it seemed long to us 7-year-olds. At the end of the prayer all adults reached for their chair and proceeded to sit down. The children were all escorted to the kitchen where a special table waited for us, which fit our size perfectly. However, we would always talk about the day when we all would be sitting at the grand dinner table.

However, now that I think about it when I finally moved from the kitchen to the main dining room it wasn't all that I thought it would be. I had to fix my own plate and wait for others to start eating. Our tea glasses were sitting in crystal holders, which were supposed to keep some sort of wet stains off the starched white tablecloth. Trying to eat and drink at the same time could be tricky, especially if you missed putting your glass back in the holder. The food sure didn't taste any different. Don't get me wrong, it was still delicious, but somehow it wasn't the same. This goes to show you that it takes a lifetime to realize that in some instances "change and all that implies" certainly isn't all that it's cracked up to be! However, "family traditions" are what Thanksgiving Day is all about! Although in my case, moving from one room to another didn't seem like a big step, it certainly was!

CHRISTMAS IN THE FIFTIES
WITH DEAR OLD CAPTAIN DAD!

Merry Christmas! Here I am early Christmas morning with a doll in hand, eyes closed half asleep, and just happy as can be that daddy didn't catch Santa Clause! That flash that you see in the background was made by a Brownie Kodak Camera!

As a child, like most, I loved Christmas. I knew that Santa Clause was the real thing and that hopefully he was going to visit my house. Every year my father would tell all of us children that he was going to set a trap to catch old Saint Nick. In this department I wasn't too popular with the neighborhood kids. This was since Daddy was a great hunter and could possibly set a trap that just might work. So, as you can see, we were all in a dilemma at Christmas time.

We would talk about it among ourselves and come up with some convincing reasons why we shouldn't worry too much about Daddy's old trap. The number one reason was that we knew for a fact that Santa was very smart. So therefore, he would see right through any trap. The other and best reason was that we knew for a fact was that if Santa could get into houses without chimneys, he could easily escape. After a few minutes us six-year-olds would get tired of worrying about this and basically forgot about it. At least until Daddy brought it up again, which was quite often on Christmas Eve!

As an only child I was very fortunate to get lots of things during the year. So therefore, when Christmas arrived, I needed more, after all a child needs lots of things to survive. Back in the old days we received only a few catalogs. Not like today where your mailbox is packed full every day for months before the big event. I would always be anxiously waiting for the "Levy's" catalog to arrive. This was my Christmas list in picture form. My father would tell me that I could circle what I wanted, and he would pass it on to Santa. Now this is the funny thing. He always told me not to spend any more than $25.00 on all my gifts. So, the process of picking the toys and then adding their costs up began with hopes that what I had picked didn't go over the designated amount.

Until I got older, I didn't understand what money and Santa Clause had in common. After doing all this work and making my final decision I would hand over my picture Christmas list to Daddy. He would hopefully, as he promised, pass it on to Santa Clause. However, I never forgot for one moment that he might catch the rascal before he got to our house. I wasn't the only child worried about this.

Most people leave cookies and milk. However, my father and I decided to make a few changes. Over the years we left sardines and saltines, Vienna sausage and Ritz's, and one time we left sea rations of can cookies and jelly. As far as something to drink we left what we had on hand at the time, which could have been anything from water straight out the faucet to something that came in a bottle. It seemed that no matter what we left Santa he always seemed to eat it all.

When Christmas morning finally arrived, I jumped out of bed, ran into the living room, and got a big letdown. There weren't any presents or toys to be found. I couldn't believe Daddy had caught Santa Clause. I ran to daddy's bedroom almost in tears and woke him up. He rose up half asleep and asked, "What's wrong?" I replied, "Santa didn't come!" He quickly replied, "Oh Santa and I got to talking about fishing, eating snacks, and he left all of your presents in my closet!"

Once again, my father saved the day with just a few words putting Christmas morning back into motion!

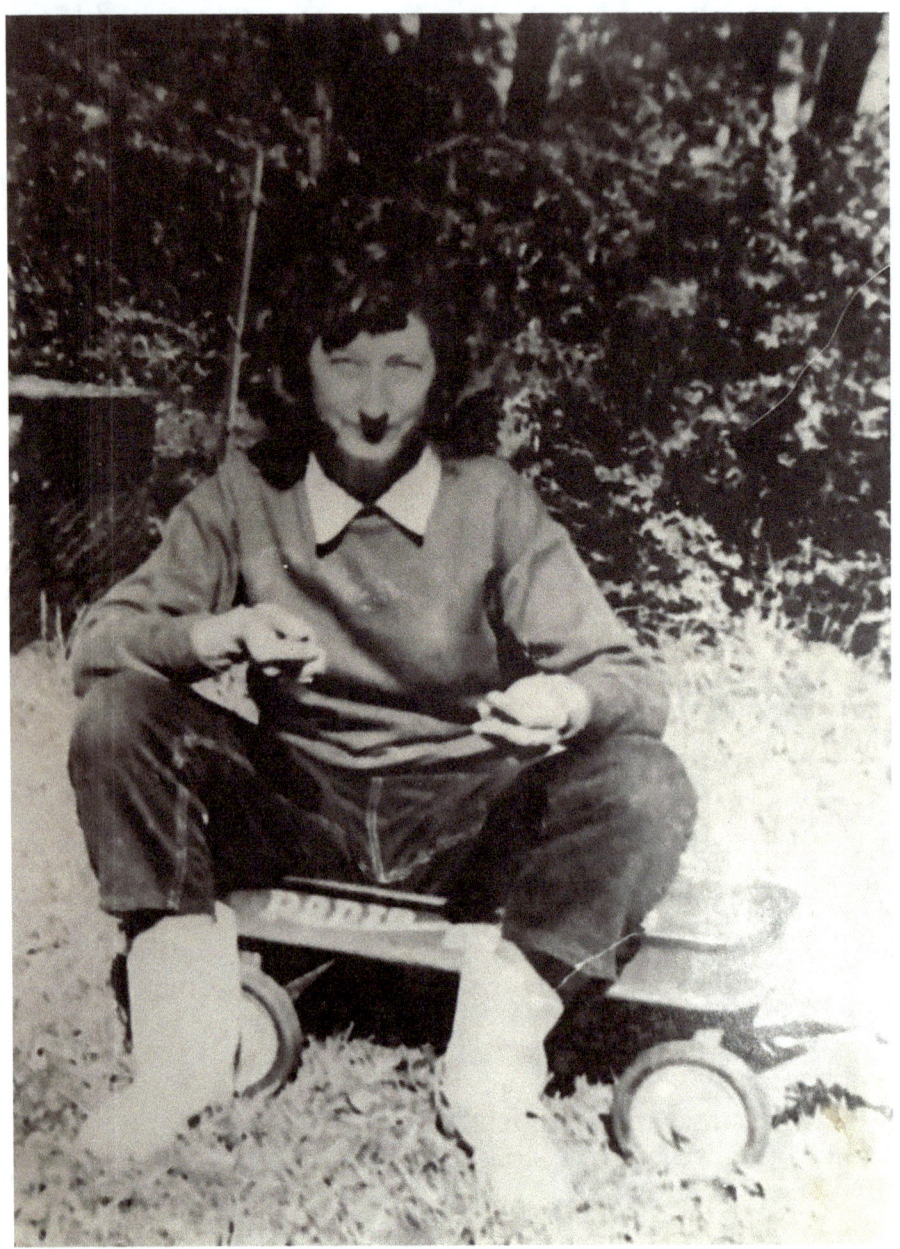

This is my mother Jerry Lovett Helmey (1925-1957). What is she sitting in? My red radio flyer wagon! She is wearing an official pair of white crabbing boots!

Extra Money

Many years ago, when I was about 8 years old, I had quite a few little businesses going on. During the summertime I would occasionally take a few people or should I say, "daddy's friends to do what's now called "Sports crabbing!" All I had to do was tie a chicken neck on the end of a string, drop over into my hot crabbing spot, and normally the crabs would come. The pay was good. I normally get $5.00 a trip. Heck, this was a good amount now that I think about it. Since I didn't have to pay for my boat, fuel, dockage, or property taxes all monies collected were mine for the keeping. Now that I think about it, "those are definitely the days to long for!" I can't say that I ran a lot of these crabbing trips, but when I did, I always got paid.

I had another small business. I used to turn in coke bottles for their deposit. I would load up my red radio flyer wagon and off to the local 7 Eleven I would go. The local store was owned by Mr. Soc. I never knew his last name. My father opened me a charge account there. It was to be used for emergencies such as miscounting the funds in my pocket when I was trying to make a purchase. At the time I didn't think to use it too much. Boy, what was wrong with me?

Most coke bottles would bring about $.02 cents. As time went on, they got as high as $.05 cents. My radio flyer would hold about two cases of drink bottles. Or should I say that was about all I could pull by myself. If I had help, they would want some of the proceeds, so I decided just to do it my darn self.

Back in my childhood days, before it was even popular, I would cut my sleeves off my shirts and pants. I loved the "raggedy look!" For me it was the in style! When you first cut your sleeves or pants off, they didn't really look very cool until they were washed a few times. Upon washing the fringes would develop, which is the look I loved. I must have looked bad, because one day while pulling my painted radio flyer wagon full of old coke bottles in my raggedy clothes someone gave me a dollar. I was puzzled at first, but then after I thought about it a new business was formed, I found out that I had an entirely different business, which was "dressing for success!"

Soc must have seen the whole thing unfold. He told my father and when he got home, boy did I get in trouble. He was mad because I had taken money in the first place, but also the fact it was from a stranger. I really didn't understand at first, my father had always told me not to take candy from strangers. He never said a thing about money!

Now you know the rest of the story!

MEETING MRS. FRANCES CHCHRAN
FOR THE FIRST TIME!

This was my Mrs. Frances Cochran. She took very good care of me for many years. And just like the way she quickly arrived she left! After thinking about this for many years it was as if her being here was a planned event. But how the heck could that have been? It seems now that I have turned 70 and while looking back that a lot of my life was somehow planned indirectly for me.

On this day I was not with daddy on the boat! I was home alone, but the Bridges 'our next-door neighbors also helped care for me were just a few footsteps away! As I was playing in the yard, I heard a car drive up. As I looked up, I saw the strangest car ever. I immediately called it the faded green Mister Bubble Car! You couldn't tell the front from the back, and it had a big bubble shaped top. The driver's door creaked open and a very strange lady looking out. She was a little on the short side, her hair was thinning red, and she had no eyebrows, but had painted on some using a pencil or crayon.

Of course, I smiled and said hello, can I help you? And she replied, "I am Francis Cochran, and I guess your father did not tell you about my arrival today!" I answered,

231

"No ma'am!" Then Mrs. Cochran told me that she had answered the ad in the newspaper about us wanting to hire a live-in housekeeper. All I could think was now we were getting somewhere. So therefore, the stranger danger situation was taken directly off the table!

Mrs. Cochran's preferred eyebrow pencil color. These were the ones that she used to paint her eyebrows on. Now don't get me wrong I do know that many women and sometimes men had to draw on their eyebrows. However, as a child I was not aware of such things, so this information was, to say the least oh so fascinating! Boy, if Mrs. Cochran only knew that in the future people would have their lips and eyebrows permanently colored. Now that I think about it and know what I learned while Mrs. Cochran was living here, I am sure she already knew as well as already had visited the future! After all anybody that can communicate with the dead could certainly time travel.

My father would put an ad in the newspaper for a life as a housekeeper, they would come to the house or he would meet them, either date them or almost marry them. It was just how it was. (Had I been old enough to understand, I would have thought daddy is putting an ad in the newspaper to attract women!) However, although I had just met Mrs. Cochran, she

232

didn't seem to be here for a boyfriend or looking for a husband. When Mrs. Cochran said, "She was here to help me, for some reason I truly believed her!" As time when on I learned for sure that Frances Cochran was not like anyone I have ever met before! So as if she had known me forever, she said, "Help me with my things!" And this is where our relationship began! As I am writing this, I have to say that where Mrs. Cochran was concerned the scenario then was kind of like the making of a movie meaning planned and not real!

I helped her unload her car! To this day, I must wonder how she got all this stuff to fit in Mr. Bubble Car. It took us over ten trips to get it all in her room. She had framed photographs, books, clothes, shoes, a set of dishes, silverware, and glasses that were cleaned with empty jelly jars. As I helped her hang up her dresses, I couldn't help but notice all the flashy cocktail gowns that she had. I smiled and touched every one of them. Mrs. Cochran asked, "You like them, don't you?" I replied, "Yes!" And then I asked would she try on a few?" She replied, "Of Course!"

I watched as she tried on each dress, and it seemed that all of them had a special memory for her. About that time, as the fashion show was just getting started Daddy walked into the living room. He smiled and greeted Mrs. Cochran and said, "Don't let me stop your fun!" With that, Mrs. Cochran kept on trying on dresses and modeling them for both of us! She even told us a few stories about dresses. It was lots of fun for sure!

It seemed that every time Mrs. Cochran tried on one of her dresses it transformed her back into the moment. Every dress had a story and had been to a fancy event, in which she remembered every detail. It sounded and from the smile delivered that her past times were wonderful. The dresses once tried on, if not for a short moment, took her back in time! I guess you could say, "Mrs. Cochran was a time traveler!"

I didn't realize this until daddy walked in, but he had not met Mrs. Cochran either. They met on the phone and from the conversation they had Daddy felt like hiring her was the right thing to do. In the many days to come Mrs. Cochran and I became very good friends. We talked about everything and believed me she knew a lot of interesting things.

233

These pictures were sent to by her Granddaughter Cindy... It has been a long time, but I have seen these jewelry boxes before. She used to keep them on the dresser in her bedroom when she lived with us. You see, she and I shared a bathroom, which was located between the two bedrooms. Occasionally I would sneak into her room and look in her jewelry boxes. I know she wouldn't have cared.

I remember just like yesterday when Mrs. Cochran would hear a song how she would quietly snap her finger while making a few dancing moves. You see, she was a big follower of Authur Murray's studios.

Mrs. Cochran and her Ballroom Dancing friend! She had her signature dance style, and it was great!

Mrs. Cochran was a member of the Arthur Murray Dance Program!

Mrs. Cochran's tourist home! She quite often had a lot of strange tenants! By the time that Mrs. Cochran started working for us her tourist home had been put on the real estate market. She had a few renters, but her goal was to sell and get out of the tourist rental business! But the stories she told about her renters were unbelievable. After spending years with Mrs. Cochran I did later for a fact, believe everything, she said was the darn absolute truth.

Mrs. Cochran owned a big boarding house on Montgomery Street, which during this time, was a very big deal. The fact of the matter is, she still owned it at this time and was trying to sell it. We would often ride by just to check it out! I loved the interesting stories about the various assortments of people that she had staying with her, especially the ones about the circus people! Heck, she even had a bearded lady stay with her a couple of times.

According to Mrs. Cochran the most interesting tenants were the families of gypsies, because they taught her how to read cards. And this is when she learned of certain powers that she never knew about having. They also aided her in honing her abilities to be able to see into the future and communicating with the dead. When she talked about seeing into the future or communing with the afterlife, I truly believe she only told me the good not the bad things. At least at first...

COCHRAN TOURIST HOME . . . Savannah, Ga. . . . U. S. 80 and 17 Highways.

Then there was this time where she saw a car moving down the street that turned into a coffin on wheels. According to the story told this only lasted a few seconds. However, when the news came on that evening it was clear that the wrecked car that killed all the people inside was the same vehicle. This is when she started semi sharing some of her thoughts. She also told me about the time that a close friend had passed, and they had tried to contact her. However, she did not response, because she was just not ready.

I wish I could remember all the stories that she told me about her renters. I can't remember how many rooms she rented, but it must have been quite a few. The board house was very big. One time she rented a room to a person who had been traveling with the circus. The person paid in full and said they were very tired, they had been on the road a lot, and they planned to sleep until they felt rested. So, Mrs. Cochran was not so concerned for the first 2 days, but at the end of the third she started smelling a strange odor. She knocked on the door and couldn't get any response. Now concerned that something might be wrong, she got the spare key and opened the door. And this not so recognizable smell overwhelmed her.

It was very dark; after entering the room she turned the light on. And what she saw then made Mrs. Cochran gasp for air. Her

236

new tenant was lying across the radiator, from the looks, the mess on the floor, and the smell they had been there for a while.

After contacting the authorities and dealing with answering all the must be asked questions the cleaners or should I say, "The removers of the half-cooked body did their job!" According to Mrs. Cochran, even after the room was cleaned and re-cleaned the now most recognizable odor still lingered.

So, it was decided that maybe a fresh coat of paint might do the job. Well, according to Mrs. Cochran, this worked, but not for long. It was decided to open the windows in the apartment and temporarily seal the door for at least a month or until the smell is gone. Mrs. Cochran never told me whether the smell had disappeared. I wish I had asked her, but I did not!

You know it's so funny now that I think about all of this. As a small child, right after my mother died, I had told my father about seeing my mother and even talking to her more than a few times. There was another time, when I was about thirty, that I came face to face with my mother. I will have to say, this scared me at first. However, afterwards I got to thinking that we were the same height! Then there was the time with my Friend Jackie Sommers had gone to the back bathroom and upon his return he asked, "Who was the lady in the back room sitting on the bed with long dark hair?" Of course, all of us in the kitchen knew there were no others in the house. However, Kathy Brown, Alli DeYoung, and I all said at the same time, "It must have been Jerry!" (Judy's mother passed away many years ago) I also remember the time that Katy Goettler told me that she had a conversation with my mother! I could go on, but I think you get the just of all of this. My mother, whether you believe in people coming back to visit after they pass or not, was here! There were too many accounts made by quite a few close friends of mine. And if I mentioned every time I saw her, we would be here for a while! I remember these things like they only happened yesterday.

So, since I knew that Mrs. Cochran had all these abilities it wouldn't have been unusual for me to ask about my mother. I told her of the times when I thought my mother was present. Mrs. Cochran always listened to what I had to say and tried to answer my questions, which were most normal if you think about it. I would always ask, "Why is she still here?" And Mrs. Cochran would always say, "She is watching over you!" And believe me that I truly think that she had a conversation with my mother. Mrs. Cochran was always so sincere about what she was saying as if she was told this information for a fact.

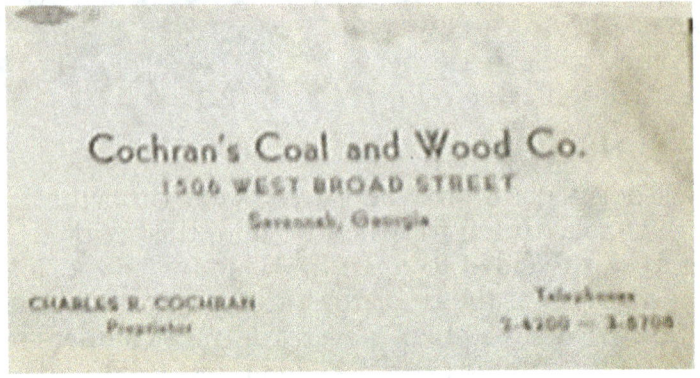

Cochran's Coal and Wood Co.
1506 WEST BROAD STREET
Savannah, Georgia

CHARLES R. COCHRAN
Proprietor

Telephones
3-4200 — 3-8706

This was Mrs. Cochran's husband's business card. Apparently, Mr. Cochran's business did quite well. They owned a large boarding house on Mongomery Street, Hill Top Cottage on the saltwater at Estill Hammock, Tybee Island, and a coal/wood company. And from all the ballroom dresses along with the memories Mrs. Cochran had it sounded like this couple was continuously on the move!

THE HILL TOP COTTAGE

When I visited Mrs. Cochran's Hill Top Cottage (it had a sign and Everything!) It was an adventure for sure. As I looked at the cottage way up on the hill in front of me, it looked like one heck of a climb. There were buried prefect size rocks that marked the path that led the way. As long as you stayed balanced on them you would be going forward not falling backwards. I could tell Mrs. Cochran had done this before. She started her ascend I closely followed. Heck, this was a lot of fun to a 9-year-old!

Inside there were all sorts of nautical things from old oars to shells. There was a dock, but I was told that I could not go out on it. It seems you had to go down the steep backside of the hill that the house was sitting on to get to the dock. I do remember it was in bad repair. However, someone had taken a lot of time and put a lot of thought into building the deck off the back of the cottage and then incorporating the dock. Although it was very run down, it did seem that at one time lots of good times and parties were had there!

I remember one time that she told me that a friend had recently passed and had tried to contact her. Mrs. Cochran said that she could hear her friend calling her name, but the voice was somewhat muffled and was very far away. Apparently, this was Mrs. Cochran's first experience with the afterlife, because she told me that she closed her mind to the calls. As I stood there in her Hilltop Cottage kitchen, I could feel something but wasn't sure and then the thought left me. I was a young child with many desires to just keep moving.

During this time Mrs. Cochran must have sold her boarding house on Montgomery Street, because I remember, just like it was yesterday, going with my father and her to this big eerie house with big windows, high steeples, and many floors. In the back of the house were more apartments and a large garage, which were all full of the stuff that must have been in the big house at one time or the other. Of course, she offered us anything that we wanted and of course my father thanked her for the generous offer and suggested she try to sell all this stuff. And now that I am older, I bet that there were antiques galore, lots of actual real silverware and plates that would have been worth lots of money sooner or later. (Furniture with claw feet, free standing bathtubs, antique light fixtures, and I could go on, but I think you get the picture!) Also back in the real old days, ladies not knowing what to do with silver after it turned green quite often just threw it away! I think this is just about when so-called garage sales became so popular especially to those that knew the southern stupidity deal!

Mrs. Cochran could read cards, tell your fortune, commune with the dead, foresee the future, and see signs that meant certain things only to her. Please don't think her or I are crazy! You know this stuff is too good to make up. And I do believe she came to my house for a reason, because I really don't know how this story would have gone if she hadn't.

Some of the stuff she told me was so interesting. And as she spoke I either vision in my mind what she was saying, or I saw it. I remember one time she told me that she was sitting in a large room with others (maybe family members or not) and that they were all in grief, due to the fact, that someone was in the bedroom next to them was on their death bed. She then told me that suddenly, a small creature (only she could hear and maybe see) ran up to the door of the bedroom and down into where they were all sitting. The fact of the matter was the creature ran across the floor, stopped briefly in front of her, and then continued until it ran right through the wall. But of course, no one could see this happening but her. (And me, but I wasn't ever there!) As soon as this happened, she already knew before everyone in the room that the person in the bedroom had passed. Now, I know you are going to think I am crazy, but in my mind, I saw this happen! And still see it. And I wasn't even there!

This is the yellow page ad that Mr. Cochran ran in the year 1952!

46   COAL DEALERS

Cochran's Coal & Wood Yard

COAL

CHARLES R. COCHRAN, JR.

1506 West Broad St.   Tel. 2-4200

240

GETTING RID OF THOSE AWFUL WARTS!

I was training to be a professional water skier!

During the sixties and seventies, I did a lot of water skiing, and it was during this era that I had lots of warts. These warts didn't like being soaked in saltwater and became very painful after a long day of skiing! And since I had so many ...

When I was very young my father hired a wonderful lady to work for us. Frances Cochran was her name, and her main job was to take care of me. I could write story after story about all the interesting things that we did and talked about. However, this is my favorite one of all times. As a child I was covered with warts from my elbows to my knees to my hands. My father had taken me too many doctors, who tried to cut or burn them off. This painful process only lasted until the colony of warts grew back. The doctors just couldn't get rid of them and believe me they tried, because I was there for every unfortunate second of this painful process. Thank goodness that Mrs. Cochran finally spoke up. One day while we were sitting in the kitchen, she made mention that she had a remedy for getting rid of warts. I was "all ears" as soon as she said it. I listened as she told me of the necessary steps that had to be taken to preempt the wart removing process. Here are the steps at least as well as I can remember them.

You need to take (yourself) an Idaho potato and cut it in half. Take half of the potato and quarter that part. I almost forgot it's very important that you perform these small tasks in the kitchen. You will need to get yourself a well-used, in other words, an old but clean dish towel. Pick up one of the quarter pieces and rub the flat edge all over your warts.

According to Mrs. Cochran it was necessary to rub all the warts that you wanted totally removed. Take the used quarter of the potato and lay it edge up slap-dab in the middle of the laid-out dishtowel. Wrap your potato part up in the dishtowel. Now you have a rolled-up potato in an old dishtowel. This is important. Take the rolled-up potato, walk outside, and head over to the neighbor's yard. You need to bury your potatoes in the ground in your neighbor's yard. I really didn't have any trouble with this; because our neighbors only visited, and they didn't live there full time. And sneaking next door and digging a small hole wouldn't be a problem.

According to Mrs. Cochran you had to bury the potato wrapped in the dishtowel in a spot that couldn't be seen from the kitchen window. This was another important part of the task. Once you dig a small hole, put your potato in the hole, and cover it up. Your next and last task is too simply to walk off and not look back. Not looking back was the hardest thing at least for me. And I had to wonder how I was never going to look that way again.

However, Mrs. Cochran eased my thoughts by saying, "After entering the kitchen the deal was sealed!" According to the rules you could not ever look at the burial site from your kitchen window. She was a smart woman and had planned it well. You couldn't, even if you wanted to, look at the burial spot from our kitchen window anyway! And how do I know this, I tried and tried and tried!

*Sorry for the redundancy but I wanted to make sure for those that might want to try that they would have the absolute step by step process. These steps are a must to do and are your best shot at getting this to work.

Wart synopsis: It took the warts exactly two weeks to totally disappear. The next morning all the warts looked as if someone had taken life out of them. They hadn't changed color or anything, they just looked different. The whole thing was so funny. They didn't fall off, they simply peacefully sunk back into my skin. That's about the only way I know to describe it. It took me less than fifteen minutes to perform the tasks, which prompted my warts to be gone!

The moral of this story is as simple one: In this case a potato is not just a potato!

It's true that the Idaho's are known for making a great mess of homemade mash potatoes, but don't think for one moment that this is all that they can do especially in the "wart removal department." If you have unwanted warts and want to try this, you certainly don't have to tell anyone. After all, all you must lose is your unwanted warts!

Please meet Frances Cochran's grandchildren Murray Cochran and his brother Chris!

I will never forget the first time I met Murry and Chris. They were in a group that had chartered my boat for an offshore 10-hour snapper boat trip. When they introduced their last name was Cochran, which stuck with me so much that I never really heard anyone else's on the boat full titles. About an hour into our ride, I had to ask. Are you guys related to Frances Cochran? And they replied, "She is our grandmother!" I almost fell off my helm chair!

243

A million questions came to mind, but as I asked, they didn't have any answers!

The reason is they did not spend any time with their grandmother. More secrets to add to the already so-called complicated life of Grandmother Frances!

The best news I can share is the fact they wish they could have spent more time, but I guess you could say, "It wasn't in the cards!"

MELDRIM TRAIN DISASTER

In June of 1959 I was asked to go as a friend of the family to a big picnic. The area where this was to take place was on the Ogeechee River where the train trestle was in the small town of Meldrim. It was an area on the river where children could swim, play together, and families while cooking out could socialize in the great outdoors. Everything was arranged! I was so excited about going I could wait to jump off the trestle. And then I heard Mrs. Cochran tell my father that she did not want me to go. My father asked why and all she could say is "Please don't let Judy go!" After talking with Mrs. Cochran my father changed his mind. And I was so very disappointed!

At 3:40 PM June 29, 1959, The Seaboard Air Line Freight Train No. 82 pulling 124 cars came rumbling over the trestle in Meldrim. On this afternoon a coupling on the car near the end of the train broke, sending the last two cars toppling into the river below. No one was injured by the falling cars. The two cars were carrying 10,000 gallons of butane gas. When the tank started leaking gas, an eerie fog formed on the water. When the gas reached an open fame, it ignited creating a raging inferno killing 14 people, injuring dozens, and reducing a 5-acre area to a pile of ash in a matter of minutes!

Mrs. Cochran stayed with us a few more years and she left about the same way she came. When it was time for her to go, she packed the Mister Bubble Car and off she went down the dirt road. You know it is funny I never saw her again, but I thought of her often. I thought that I might see her again sometime, but I have not so far. But if you think about it, especially in this case, time has no boundaries!

OLD CRAZY JACK WAS GOOD AS GOLD!

Crazy Jack Gilmore 1933-2021 and Captain Judy Helmey

If he liked you, you could go on and like him, but it was his choice! And I was proud he liked me! I remember back in the seventies I would stop by his place Crazy Jacks Records and Tapes store on DeRenne. And believe me we had some fun. You see there was a back room and in the back room was a reversed mirror. I think that is what they are called. In other words, you could see the person in the mirror, but they couldn't see you!

Bottle Necking and maybe peeing in your pants!

This normally took place when he was alone in the store. We would head to a secret storage area and wait to see what was going to happen. When a potential customer came in and couldn't find a clerk, it seemed they would always start what Crazy Jack called "bottle necking!" These were the ones that were just thinking

247

about taking something, but they didn't! Then there were others that might have thought about grabbing something and running but they did not! Crazy Jack would always say, "I guess the big gun news got around quick. I pulled the gun out and almost pointed it at the person that was trying to steal something!" According to story told Crazy Jack let the so-called shoplifter run out the door. However, their hands were empty, and he was sure they might have been peeing in their pants!

Crazy Jack and Uncle Bobby just a singing! Oh My!

Over the years I got to spend some wonderful times with Crazy Jack. He attended my 50th birthday party, which went down in history as one of those unforgettable evenings! My father would have been so proud of me! Once Crazy Jack started talking with Uncle Bobby (also his good friend) things in the entertainment department got wild for sure! We had a karaoke machine with all the trimming. And the person, or should I say the DJ of the Karaoke was dressed to the nines just like Evis Presley! So crazy for sure!! And this my friend is a great story for my next book! And it will go something like this several hundred people arrived at my 50Th Birthday party and you aren't going to believe what happened! Stay tuned!

248

I think what I love most of all was the fact that Crazy Jack was always the same person no matter what! To understand this is to know Crazy Jack as a friend! I love me some Crazy Jack!!

My friend, Crazy Jack wasn't so CRAZY as he was JUST PLAIN COOL!

The last and best of its kind! I know the family will do a great job of keeping it between the lines!

CAPTAIN KATHY BROWN
AND HER MOTHER MRS. WILMA BROWN

Mrs. Wilma Brown 1923-2005 She is sitting on my father's boat "Miss Jerry" holding a spool of line. Mrs. Wilma loved to go boat riding and see all the waterfront mansions.

Mrs. Wilma Brown and her Statesboro Friends!

Bumpy roads, drug traffickers, red headed professional gamblers, and not- rental cars!

This is a true story about friendships, trust, knowledge, people with all kinds of authority, know-how, clump of pine trees, mile long bumpy back dirt roads, a convicted red headed drug trafficker, professional gamblers, and five almost new, but not rental cars.

Every time I think about Mrs. Wilma Brown, also known as Mrs. Wilma, I get a smile on my face. She was probably one of the strongest women that I have ever met. She raised two children all alone and did a great job of doing it. She had a daughter and a son. Her daughter is my long-time friend as well as my first mate on the Miss Judy Too, Captain Kathy Brown. Mrs. Wilma also had a son named Mike. Mrs. Wilma lived in Statesboro and was known far and wide by those that lived and worked in the area. From the politicians to the police department to the drug dealers they chased, Mrs. Wilma was in the know. Now I must add that Mrs. Wilma had family/friends with possible long-time ties with the local police department, FBI, and alleged drug traffickers, and professional gambling rings.

When I first met Mrs. Wilma, I will never forget that wonderful smile on her face. You couldn't help but instantly like her. For many years our families got together on holidays and at all sorts of functions. I felt like and considered Mrs. Wilma part of my extended family. She had lots of qualities such as no job was too hard, and she was one of the best cooks I have ever seen. When you visit Mrs. Wilma's dinner table, she always cooks a special dish for each of her guests. My favorite was creamed silver queen corn. Believe me when I say, "I could make an entire meal on just eating her creamed corn!"

Every time I passed through Statesboro, I always tried to stop by and say "hello!" On this night around 10:00 PM I was on my way to Augusta to see some friends. As soon as I made the turn near Mrs. Wilma's Street to get to the west side of Statesboro my car had a serious mechanical malfunction. Apparently, the power steering hose felt the need to bust, which was a very bad thing. However, when the worst comes it brings on some good times, which after reading this you will most likely have to agree! Now here's the thing…if my power steering hose hadn't busted, I would have never got to experience such a wonderful ordeal!! Believe me, I am still talking about this over thirty-year old adventure today!!

So here I am, it's around 10:00 PM and my car has broken down. As soon as that thought ran through my head Mrs. Wilma's name popped into my mind. The best news was that her house was less than a half mile away. So, I fought with the steering until I reached Mrs. Wilma's driveway. As I made the turn up in her front yard, I could see lights on and her small new blue car in the driveway. Before I could get out of the car Mrs. Wilma met me on the porch with a big smile and wave.

Mrs. Wilma is opening a gift that was hand delivered by good old Saint Nick!

After a big hug was received, I started telling Mr. Wilma what had happened to my car. By this time, it was around 11:00 PM and I knew no local car rental shops would be open. As we talked, Mrs. Wilma offered to lend me her car so that I could get where I was going, which was very nice of her. However, I needed somewhat more permanent transportation fix, and I didn't want her to be without a car for even one night.

As we talked Mrs. Wilma said, "You know I just might know someone that can help us." It was getting close to midnight, but that didn't seem to make a difference to Mrs. Wilma Brown! We headed out the door and began a most unbelievable adventure. As soon as we got down the steps Mrs. Wilma handed me the keys and said, "You drive, and I will tell you where to go!" So, I cranked up, backed up, and started taking driving directions. I am not sure what main road we turned off. However, I am sure that from this point we were on a very dark dirt road for many a mile. About 5 miles into the dirt road ride, Mrs. Wilma said, "Now slow down a bit and let me get my bearings!" I slowed a bit and watched as she pointed, recanted, pointed, recanted, and then said; "This isn't the turn." So, I picked up speed to about 20 miles per hour riding over yet another dirt road mile. It's my opinion that a dirt road mile and a paved road mile, even though the measurements are identical, are two different animals. Dirt

252

roads have plenty of bumps and holes. As we rode bumpy bump it reminded me somewhat of riding waves on the ocean.

As we rode Mrs. Wilma talked about how long it had been since she had been in the neck of the woods. I had my bright lights on so that I could see anything that was in my path. So far so good! All at once Mrs. Wilma said, "Turn left right after you pass that clump of pine trees." Sure enough, there was a dirt road to the left, which after the turn had the same terrain as the one, we just turned off. This road was lined with trees and shrubs on both sides. Two automobiles could pass, but it would be a little close encounter, for sure. When we got to the end of the road there was a large house with all the lights on. We got out, walked up to the house, and the door opened and out came "Red." Walking towards us with open arms he hugged Mrs. Wilma and said, "It's good to see you!"

The man meeting us in the yard was of medium build, nice looking, clean cut, and his hair was red. Hence the name Red was the name that I gave him. I was introduced but can't remember his name to this day. So, the conversation began like this. Mrs. Wilma said, "Judy's car broke down and she needs to rent one until she can get hers fixed." Red replied, "There are plenty of cars outside (5 to be exact!) with the keys in them and you can take your pick!" While all this conversation was going on between Mrs. Wilma and Red my eyes started wondering about. It was then that I noticed there was no furniture in this house and all the rotary dial phones were basically sitting on the floor. The room that we were standing in looked to have been a busy place at one time. There were scrapes and scratches on the floor as if there was some sort of heavy furniture present at one time. There also were lots of double electrical boxes and numerous empty phone jacks.

As if I had been somewhere else, I finally zoned myself back into the conversation. Red said, "Judy you can take your pick of automobiles out there. Here's a flashlight so that you can decide." I asked, "How much do I need to pay you and when?" Red said, "The car rental is $25.00 per day with unlimited mileage." This sounded like a deal to me. Then Red said, "When you get ready to return the car take it to the mechanic shop next to Mrs. Wilma's house. And if you want your car fixed, I am sure these guys will be glad to help you. The fact of the matter is

Mrs. Wilma can call them tomorrow and they can pick up your car and repair it. When you return the rental then you can pick up your car. This is the last time you will talk to me for at least 5 years. I am reporting to prison in the morning. I had to ask even though I didn't want to, it just popped out of my mouth. "What the heck for?" Red said, "Drug trafficking and gambling charges."

Mrs. Wilma relaxing on my father's charter boat, Miss Jerry!

As soon as this came out of his mouth, I knew I was standing in the place and just about to rent a car that had been at one time, or another, possibly was involved in Red's operation. In my mind I had to say, "Now how cool is that?"

Red then said, "When you want to return the car you can either pay Mrs. Wilma or the mechanic shop next to her." According to Red the mechanic shop was inadvertently his business, but only in a "say so bases! The ownership papers had another name, which was something other than Red's name. Mrs. Wilma gave Red a big hug and then he hugged me too.

As Mrs. Wilma and I cranked up our cars consecutively my mind raced to wonder how these two knew each other. As I fell in behind her making my way down the bumpy bump dirt road, I tried recapping what had just happened. I was now driving a car, which I never signed for. Not only that, but I also didn't even know if it had any insurance whatsoever. So, with that though I concurred that my current automobile policy may or may not cover an automobile that may or may not belong to a convicted drug dealer/illegal gambler or not!

By the time we got back to Mrs. Wilma's house it was around 2:00 AM. After thanking her for everything she smiled and said, "Leave me your keys and I will have your car fixed in the morning." I handed her the keys and hugged her goodbye thanking her once again. By 2:30 AM I was back on the road headed to Augusta, Georgia arriving somewhere around 4:00 AM.

I stayed in Augusta for a few days touching base with Mrs. Wilma about my car. My plans were to drop off my rental and pick up my car on the way home. Well, as luck would have it, the mechanic had to order some parts for my car. So therefore, instead of stopping to pick up my car I drove straight through Statesboro making way to Savannah.

After about three days, Mrs. Wilma called to say, "Your car is ready!"

When I arrived at Mrs. Wilma's, she instructed me to go across the street to return the rental and pick up my car. Once I got into the office, I explained who I was and that I was there to return the rental and pick up my car. No one seemed to know about the rental and there was certainly no charge. The only charge was for repairs done to my automobile. I tried on several occasions to ask about the rental. However, everything I said fell on deaf ears. So, I then asked, "What do I do with the car that I just drove up in?" They all replied, "Park it in the parking lot and leave the keys in it.

As soon as I picked up my car up I "be-lined it" over to Mrs. Wilma's house so that I could tell her about the rental. Once inside I said, "They wouldn't let me pay anything for the rental!" And Mrs. Wilma said, "What rental?" And she smiled that smile that could mean so many things!!! And I guess you could say we left it just like that!!!!

A special thanks goes out to Mrs. Wilma! She might have gone to that big place in the sky, but the memory of what she left here for us will live on forever in stories that we will never get tired of telling, much less hearing!

Young Mrs. Wilma Brown! This picture was taken in Japan late 1940's! Mrs. Wilma is ready to do some shopping in Japan!

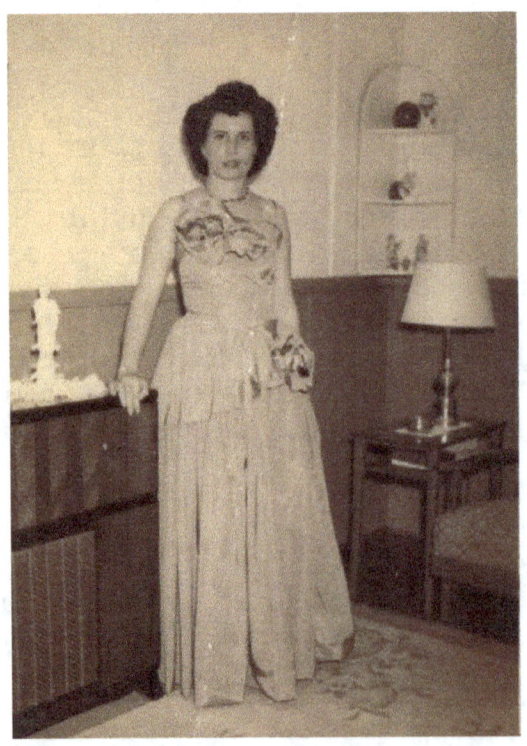

Mrs. Wilma Brown - This picture was taken in Japan late 1940's!

Captain Kathy shared a story that her mother told her many times. While Mrs. Wilma was living in Japan she found a very large spider in her closet. She trapped the 8-legged wonder in a cigar box, placed the box in open where she could watch it, and waited until her husband came home from work. Of course, when Mr. Brown arrived home, he dealt with the spider! After all Mrs. Brown had, had enough!

Not a Macrothele gigas mostly found in Japan

The spider that Ms. Brown trapped in the cigar box was most likely from the Macrothele gigas family, which is considered the largest spider in Japan.

According to the Web, there is a Japanese myth about spiders!

The jorogumo spider is said to spin silk strong enough to capture a man in her web.

And that is not all…

So, I did a little checking into old time Japan spider/insects, Sorcerers, serums, and curses.

It is written that way back when so called Sorcerers created a curse serum, called Kodoku. How was Kodoku made? The Sorcerers would mix several insects varieties in a jar, and let them kill one another, until only one survived. The fluids extracted from the only survived insect would be used to poison an individual with a curse that would control them, cause them misfortune or just plain kill them! No middle of the road here!

Captain Kathy Brown has worked with me for many years! (over 40 years and has been like family for longer than that) And the promise is she will be here until the deal is done! What does that mean? We will retire from taking people fishing at the same time. Now I am not saying we will stop entertaining people when it comes to talking about fishing, telling fish catching lies, because that will officially never end! Why? We have lots more to say!

"Words are easy, like the wind;
faithful friends are hard to find!"

~William Shakespeare!

Captain Kathy Brown and her mother Mrs. Wilma Brown (late 1970's)

Captain Kathy Brown
"Good friends are hard to find, harder to leave, and impossible to forget!"
~Captain Judy Helmey

Two old friends and a big scamp grouper!

*Captain Kathy Brown holding up a nice scamp grouper that Captain Steve
"Triple Trouble" Howell just caught, fought, and is not going to release! Why?
It is legal to keep and it's going to be dinner for many!*

Captain Kathy Brown and a big Genuine Red Snapper!

"I get by with a little help from my friends!"

~ The Beatles

We have been friends a long long time!

This is something that I really do cherish! I know that I can depend on you to be there when needed, I know that I can depend on you to guard the lane, and I also know that I am glad that you are here my dear friend!

And, when it comes to fishing, you can read my mind while we both are trying second guessing the ways of fish!

My new saying is this:

> *"Every Day is a Gift so lets make them all an adventure!*
> *And when it comes to you and me it has all been a grand adventure!"*

Yes, Captain Kathy we will go down as the best fishing team ever!

MEET JOYCE FISCHER

Picture provided by Joyce Fischer

This is Joyce Fischer! (1935-2025) She is the mother of Frankie, Jimmy, and Nash! And I consider her and the family as one of our elite Wilmington-islanders! Ms. Joyce is sharp as a tack and helped me a lot with this book! Ms. Joyce is a mother, great fisher, conning, a great first mate also know as a striker, sharp-witted, nice when needed, and properly the opposite when apporpriate! I just have always liked her so much!!

Ms. Joyce has always celebrated St. Patrick's day in Savannah. Heck, it is one of their family traditions!

Ms. Joyce Fischer and Captain Sherman I. Helmey
on the stern of the Miss Jerry!
What are they up to?
Getting ready to celebrate St. Patricks 1984 Style!

263

MS. JOYCE - DADDY'S STRIKER!

Now, over the years, during the eighties, Ms. Joyce worked on and off with my father as a first mate! (Captain Sherman I. Helmey on his boat Miss Jerry)

He was quite a card and I preferred him using males and not females. And not because one was better than the other either!

My father had a little problem when it came to his language and his sneaky ways especially around the ladies! (if you get my drift!) Ms. Joyce could and did handle my father's out of the way requests!

By the look on my father's face I truly believe sometimes he wasn't sure whether she said yes or no! She was so good that way! I guess you could say, "Ms. Joyce had my father's correct number, dailed it frenquently, and hung up a lot!"

I must add this: During his day, my father had another name for a first mate. He called them "strikers!" I remember this like it was yesterday.

Daddy would say or, should I say scream, "Judy I need a striker for tomorrow!"

FIRST MATES'S ALSO KNOWN AS STRIKERS WANTED!

While I am on the subject of first mates and strikers. I must add this bit of information. I will never forget this. This happened during the seventies!

I walked into the Savannah Bank on Crosswroads and my banker Mr. Sam McTeer said, "I read in the classified section today that you are hiring!" I know I looked puzzeled over his statement, because I really did not know what Mr. McTeer was talking about. I just smiled and after doing my banking I left. I grabbed a Savannah Morning newspaper, turned to the classified section, and yep there was an ad that my father had run.

And it went something like this: WANTED AT ONCE— female from the ages of 18 to 25 to work as a striker on my charter boat, wants a place to live, and do some light house work call 912 897 2478 (My father house phone line) The fact of the matter is I still have that land line phone number!

Most people did not see the 1993 movie Bevelry Hillbillies staring Dolly Parton, Buddy Ebsen, Jim Varney, Lily Tomlin, etc... (Just to name a few)

Well, Jethro Bodine put an ad on a busy billboard advertising for females that might be interested in applying for marrying his Millionair uncle Jed! The fire storm of applicants arrived in big waves to Milburn Drysdale bank.

Well, in our case the female applicants arrived in great number to our dock! Just like in the movie, several women arrived on motorcycles, some in boats, some walked up, drove cars, took taxis, and some brought their luggage!

This was yet another mess that I had to straighten out, which I did for sure! And what did it leave me with?

One heck of a story that I could share with you!

Ms. Joyce's sons Nash, Jimmy and Frankie

Nash Roger, Ms. Joyce's last born!

Please meet Nash Fischer Ms. Joyce Fischer's youngest son. Nash is known for sharing his great adventures, (whether the police are involved or not) retaining the past like it only happened yesterday, and if you have a cooling or heating problem he can fix it. The fact of the matter is he is one of those guys that most likely can fix anything with the things that he already has on hand! Whatever you do never rule this out!

This is Jimmy Fischer Ms. Joyce's middle son. Jimmy kept his older and younger brothers in line! And I loved that about him!

Frankie Fischer and his mother Ms. Joyce!
And what were they celebrating?
Ms. Joyce's 88th birthday!

And then there is Frankie, her first born, child...of which is very knowledgable of anything that floats! From the engines to the turning of the props that move them. Before computer programs were put into place the only way to straighten a prop, ajusted the pitch, or add a cup was to be in the know. And young Frankie was that guy. He could fix it, weld it, straighten it, and then if he had too, because it wasn't available, he would just plain design it! I must say and I will that Ms. Joyce's sons are all "Real True Macgyver's!"

Ms. Joyce's Grandson Joseph!

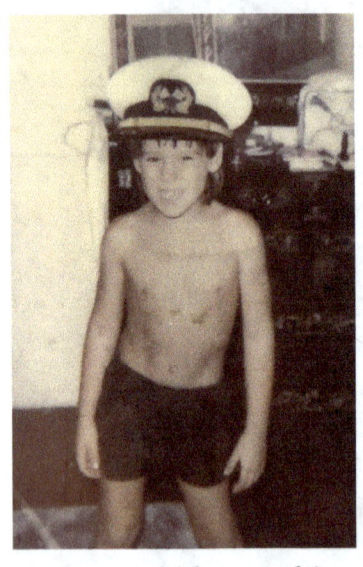

Please meet Ms. Joyce's grandson, Captain Joseph Fischer to be! He started wearing the captain's hat early, it looked good and fit even better later on! And this is how all this wanting to be a captain stuff got started!

And here we have an all grown up Captain Joseph Fischer, big time tug boat captain. He is holdng up a picture of oh so famous Flying Lady! And this is a note that he sent is Grandmother Joyce: From the first day I ever worked on a boat I knew I wanted to be a captain and I never would have achieved that goal without you and I am ever greatful! Joesph! And what do I have to say about this? Joesph is a very good appreciative grand son! Joseph's grandmother (Ms. Joyce Fischer) is just plain simply wonderful and so very in the know!

Pictures provided
by Joyce Fischer

TROUT GALORE!

I told you Ms. Joyce Fischer was a fisher, but what I really meant was she is a "LADY CATCHER OF FISH!"

And what do you call this amount a fish?

A soon to be Fish Fry that will feed so many!

Picture provided by Joyce Fischer

CAPTAIN BOYD, MS. JOYCE AND THE FLYING LADY!

Ms. Joyce told me that she loves all the memories generated while working with Captain Boyd on the Flying Lady! Some stories she could share while others can't be disclosed until after 2026. What does this mean? Ms. Joyce Fischer will be in the next published book too!

I remember Captain Boyd, like it was only yesterday, that I saw him navigating up Turner's Creek bringing the big beautiful Flying Lady by our dock. If I couldn't get to the dock to wave I would always open the sceen door and give them a shout out. And of course Captain Boyd would blow the horn, which daddy and I always loved to hear. It made both of us smile!

Captain Clifford M. Boyd (1927-2005) and Ms. Joyce Fischer (first mate) 1935-2025 standing in the wheelhouse of the impressive vessel Flying Lady! Ms. Joyce worked as a first mate for Captain Clifford for 7 wonderful years.

While they were passing our dock Captain Boyd's guests for that evening would be toasting with their coctails held high! The always waved back and they were always smiling big time! My father always said, "You know I bet those people don't know how lucky they really are to get to ride on such a beautiful boat! It is a trip that they don't think much of now, but later this event will be a subject that will control many a conversation!" According to my father, only a chosen few got to ride on the Flying Lady! In the first place, you must be some sort of special to get invited! C & S Bank aka Mills B. Lane owned the Flying Lady! (and that my friend it another story!)

Mill B. Lane, owner of The Flying Lady, personally designed this logo for the hats! This is First Mate Joyce Fischer's personal hat. What does the logo supposed to be? It's an alligator reclinning in a lounge chair holding a shaken not stirred martini! Now, I am thristy! I would prefer a Gibson! What is a Gibson? All the same alochol mix. However, instead of two olives with added olive brine it is garnished with two coctail onions only! It was my belief that back in the good old days a Martini drink seemed like a simple alocholic mixture. However, garnishments rule when it comes to name calling regarding this drink!

Picture provided by Joyce Fischer

Picture provided by Joyce Fischer

Flying Lady 1937 Trumpy 60 foot, 16.5 breadth, 4'5" draft, twin Detroit diesel 4-53N (110 horsepower each) The vessel's frames were sistered with white oak timbers. In 1998, the hull later went through a custom C-Flex fiberglass plank fabrication process. The process added strenght and renewed life to the vessel's hull!

Trumpy Yachts were known far and wide for their elaborate interior that could only apeal to rich and soon famous! These yachts were built for the purchaser that wanted long voyages with over the top comfort! And what did all of this boil down to according to my father? You got to pay and pay a lot to play this way!

The bottom line the Flying Lady was a beautiful yacht and anyone that was lucky enough to get invited to ride most likely really never forgot about it. And as they got older, I know they cherish the memory even more! I bet this subject still comes up in conversations! Now listen, don't let this subject die, just keep talking about it!

PLEASE MEET BO PEEP SILVER AND NASH ROGERS (MS. JOYCE'S FATHER)!

Picture provided by Joyce Fischer

It is my thought, just the picture itself, leans into the fact that these two fellows could be involved in some pretty interesting stuff! Nash was in charge of logistics, which meant he made sure that the product, in this case the liquior, was properly delivered! And Bo Peep sold it to those that consumed it as soon as they received it! Bo Peep's pool Hall was more than a playground for adults to drink. It was a gathering point, a hub, and a place where some stuff was delievered, but didn't gather any dust! It was a deliver in move out kind of holding spot!

Bo Peep was a pool hall proprietor, bootlegger, and bookie. He operated brazenly and notoriously in Savannah, Georgia for over 40 years. Bo's pool hall was located on Congress and Drayton! And how did he get away with this brazen attitude of doing just about any illegal thing he wanted? Bo had a partner and his name was Slim Barnes, who's brother was Sidney that just happened to be the chief of police! Need I say anymore? Just like my father always said, "Sometimes it's not what you know that gets the job done, it is who you know!" In this case, it seems, knowing the right person and then being also related to them certainly does change everything! After all everybody likes a little pocket change or should I say, "Rolls of bills in bigger denominations!"

Please Meet Ms. Joyce's mother Inez Womble and her father Nash Rogers!

From the previous picture you already know that back in the day Nash worked for Bo Peep while supplying him with the desired amount of alcohol with prefect timing.

Joyce's mother Inez was a hair dresser at the orginal Desoto Hotel. Inez along with many other hairdressers at the hotel kept the the rich and famous looking like movie stars! But that is not all that Inez was. She basically was a messenger with prejudice. (Ms. Inez is not going to talk about it since she does not know what to talk about!)

Joyce's parents Inez Womble and Nash Rogers.

Since this was long before pagers or cell phones messages had to be delieved by phone or telegraph. When delieverd by phone there was a switch board operator involved. So quite often the so called secret message was sent by telegraph. And it would read something like this: If the message delieverd by telegraph read "Inez, I will pick you up tonight!" (This meant the liquor was not being delivered tonight!) and if the message read "Inez, I will not pick you up tonight!" (This meant liquior is coming and its time to notify your buyers!)

THIS BO PEEP AIN'T NO FAIRY TALE!

This is my kind of book! If you are reading what I am writing, and like it, then you should order yourself a copy of this book! You can find it on amazon! You will not be sorry!

SEE IF YOU CAN FIND THEM!

Now this is a great picture for sure. This is Bo Peep's Billard Parlor! Where billiards was the game played and the best roast beef sandwiches were served! Heck, while you are playing pool, you must eat, drink, and be very merry! And this was the place that could deliver all the good stuff!

Boy, if I could interview a few of these guys while playing pool, eating a grand roast beef sandwich, while drinking the good stuff I would be in serious state of happiness! They all look like possible rascals to me! And racsals are broken down into three catagories.

In this picture I see 15 possible mischievous persons, 15 potential scallywags, and quite a few imps! See if you can find them! Draw a circle around the mischievous persons, a square around the scallywags, and a triangle around the imps. The correct answers are not posted upsidedown on page 27! If only pictures could talk!

ONE NIGHT AT MITCHELL'S BAR...

During the late fifties on Wilmington Island there was this bar called "Mitchell's. This was called the local watering hole by many including my father. It was built just like a log cabin. The fact of the matter is there were quite a few actual log cabins of all sizes built on Wilmington Island. Mitchells wasn't just an old bar. It was a package shop, and a grocery store complete with a separate meat display refrigerator box. Back then, I think this was the only store on Wilmington Island except for Roundtree's Service Station, but that's another story for later down the road.

When you walked into Mitchell's the first thing you came too was the grocery store, which carried all kinds of canned goods and cookie isle. Of course, an 8-year-old would be interested in this! To the left of the grocery store area there was a door, which was where the package shop was located. From the front of the store, you could see the neon lights blinking over the separate door to the package store. After getting inside it was all the same building. It just looked separate outside. Before I move on from this area I have got to tell you about the meat display refrigerator. At least that is what I called it. It was very big, and it had a glass window in front displaying the meat inside. Well, my father wanted some bologna one night, so he had Archie Mitchell, store owner and friend cut us some meat. All meats had a nice red color. When we got home with the meat, we could not eat it, because daddy said, "He had never seen brown bologna before!" This was the last time we brought meat there. We later found out that the lights in the meat display were red making everything look just perfect!!!

However, my father brought lots of other things from Mitchell's store. The fact of the matter is we were there a lot, and I spent a whole bunch of time looking at those shelves of cookies. After walking through the grocery store there was a big room with chairs and tables. On one end was a TV, which was mounted overhead in a corner. On the other end there was the biggest Moosehead that I have ever seen. It had a very large rack and a big set of black eyes, which seemed to follow me as I walked

This is a horrible picture of Mitchell's Store, but it is all I could find. It was a real-time log cabin. It had two stories. On the bottom floor was the grocery store, package shop, and bar. On the top floor was Mr. and Mrs. Mitchell's home. Check out the old gas pump!

around the room. I started to tell daddy, but I thought better of it. In the back of the room was another door which I never walked through. However, my father passed through it many times. While he was behind this door, I would always make myself at home just looking around and not trying to stare back at that big moose head hanging on the wall.

There was this one occasion where daddy told me that if I wanted to get some cookies off the shelf I certainly could. Boy, this was different. As soon as daddy passed through the door somewhere I raced to get to the cookie isle. I remember thinking, "Which cookies do I want? And how do I know?" Well, I really can't say for sure how this happened, but I started opening boxes. After all I had plenty of time. After tasting the cookies that I opened I finally found one that really got my attention. It was kind of like a Vanilla wafer that we know today. However, each cookie was a sandwich made with a marshmallow smashed in the middle. There were so very good too!!

When my father finally came back through the door, there I was sitting on the shelf with all the open boxes of cookies. It wasn't until then that I figured out that I might have done something wrong. Well, my father looked at all the boxes and then asked Mr. Mitchell, "How much do I owe you?" My father picked me up and Mr. Mitchell counted the open boxes of cookies. Then he paused and said, "You know I have some big glass jars over there that I keep cookies in. I will just dump all of them into the jars." The only thing you owe me for was the boxes of cookies, which are in Judy's hand. Little did or maybe he knew, but I think Mr. Mitchell most likely saved me from being put on "a restriction of no more cookies!"

Many years ago, Homer and I got to talk about old times. Well, Mitchell's Store came up in the conversation and Homer's eyes widened. And then he told me this story about my father...

Philip James and "World Famous" meditator Homer Collins
1940-2012

WORLD FAMOUS HOMER COLLINS
CURTAILED THE IMPENDING ONE-SIDED FIGHT!

According to Homer he had stopped at Mitchell's to pick up something before heading home and he heard some noises coming from the back room. Homer said, "The noises weren't on a friendly note." So therefore, he walked into the back room and as he did, he saw a man busting a beer bottle over the edge of the table. Homer, then hollowed "hey now!" and the man turned with broken beer bottle in hand and said, "This is none of your business!" Homer said, "I am making it my business!" No sooner did this come out of his mouth did he notice that my father was the other man. According to Homer my father wasn't excited, nor did he look angry. Not only that, but he didn't look scared either.

Now Homer knew he had to be the mediator to get this one-sided battle stopped. According to Homer, Daddy just sat there smiling like an "old Chessy Cat," which seemed to even anger the man holding the bottle even more. Homer quickly stepped in and said, "You really don't want to do this even if you think it is necessary!" As soon as a third party was added it seemed like the man with broken bottle had lost a little of his beating up desires.

Although this is the worst copy of a picture ever... if you look closely, you will see my father sporting his old signature "Old Chessy Cat smile!"

It was all about her liking me more!

As Homer and I talked he said, "Your father never broke a smile, and he didn't even say anything!" As Homer talked to man that wanted to fight a bit of his anger was lost. Then it seemed the man with the broken bottle couldn't get out of the door fast enough. At this time my father said, "Hey, Homer can I buy you a drink?" They sat for a while and talked. And of course I had to ask, "What did daddy say about the man?" Homer replied with a somewhat of his own "Old Chessy Cat smile…Your father said, "It was all about her liking me more!" (If you knew my father, you would have had to like him and then love him even more! That's just how it was back then!)

So therefore, thanks to great meditations of "the world-famous Homer Collins" there was no one sided duel created while trying to handle my daddy's old school habits!!!

Good looking Homer Collins, Jr (1940-2012)
A successful mediator!

281

This is not the machine gun that Mr. Homer showed me, but it sure did look like this one! This is a picture I took while attending the grand opening of the American Prohibition Museum! My father Gangster Captain Sherman I. Helmey has his own corner dedicated to his mafia shenanigans!

A TRUE VINTAGE MACHINE GUN!

After 17 1/2 years of service Homer retired from Chatham County Police Department. He drove the first mobile crime lab to Savannah! And then he did many fun things!

I wished I had gotten a picture of this! Mr. Collins showed me one of his pride and joy pieces from his gun collection, which came straight from the 1930's ERA! As he was holding this vintage machine gun, I knew that one of the old gangsters must have owned it and gifted it to Mr. Homer!

Who knows, Mr. Homer might have helped one of his gangster friends like he did my father. After all we know that he was very good at being a successful meditator! What is the meaning of a successful meditator? No punches delivered!

THE UNCLE BOBBY AKA "REDS" SAID...

The rattle snake, stuffed, and sitting on Archie's bar could still deliver a serious bite!

One night at Mitchell's bar! You already know that Mitchell's store was somewhat of a local watering hole and a place where lies and legends most likely got started! So, my Uncle Bobby aka REDS author of "Lemon Dance" and confirmed high-jacker emailed me some very interesting information regarding Archie's Mitchell's store.

A must read!

According to Reds' story, Mitchell's was a great place to visit and lots of folks would stop by on their way home from work. On a counter in the store was large stuffed rattle snake, which Archie had killed on Wilmington Island. Archie had it stuffed to make people aware of the serious snake population on the Island. Archie said, "It might help people to be aware of where they stepped!" When Uncle Bobby told me about the snake, I could not remember seeing that snake. However, after I thought about it that snake was most likely right there, but my father never brought it to my attention. Since my father was deathly afraid of snakes, he might have thought that it would have caused me to have nightmares.

Pretend this is a stuffed rattlesnake sitting on a counter and looking straight at you...and if it bites you in this scenario here's the cure...Please don't try this cure with regular live rattlesnake bites! Why? I don't think it will work!

MITCHELL'S BAR ANTIVENOM!

At any rate, Archie owner of Mitchell's, killed a snake on Wilmington Island and it was a big one, too.

According to Uncle Bobby it looked so real that you might jump if you hadn't thought about it being there on the counter. Uncle Bobby told me that this poor dead as well as stuffed rattle snake became involved in many a cover up story.

There was this one time that a local had stopped by for a few beers and ended up having more than usual. When he finally arrived home late while being completely intoxicated his wife asked where the heck have you been? Well, he said, "I was at Archie's aka Mitchells having a few beers, when the snake on the counter bit me.

Archie told me about the only antivenom for this snake bite was to drink at least 13 Pabst Blue Ribbon Beers. Since I had already drank two, I went on and had 11 more as quick as I could!"

And now you know a little about how life went on Wilmington Island!!!

CHARACTERS AND PLACES MENTIONED

288

290

Red fish aka spot tail bass

If you would like to give fishing a try…
Miss Judy Charters offer both inshore and offshore fishing!
The best news is that we have been in business since 1948!
So, we must know what we are doing!
Call the office - 912 897 4921

Meet Bubbles!

We are also offering guided tours/dolphin watching.

What does this boil down too? The sites, the stories are always available, and sometimes the dolphins are too!

We have four named dolphins in our creek. I hope you get to meet Bubbles, Scar, Popeye, and Captain Ryan!

Miss Judy Charters 912 897 4921

www.missjudycharters.com